This book belongs to :

____

____

Color Test Page

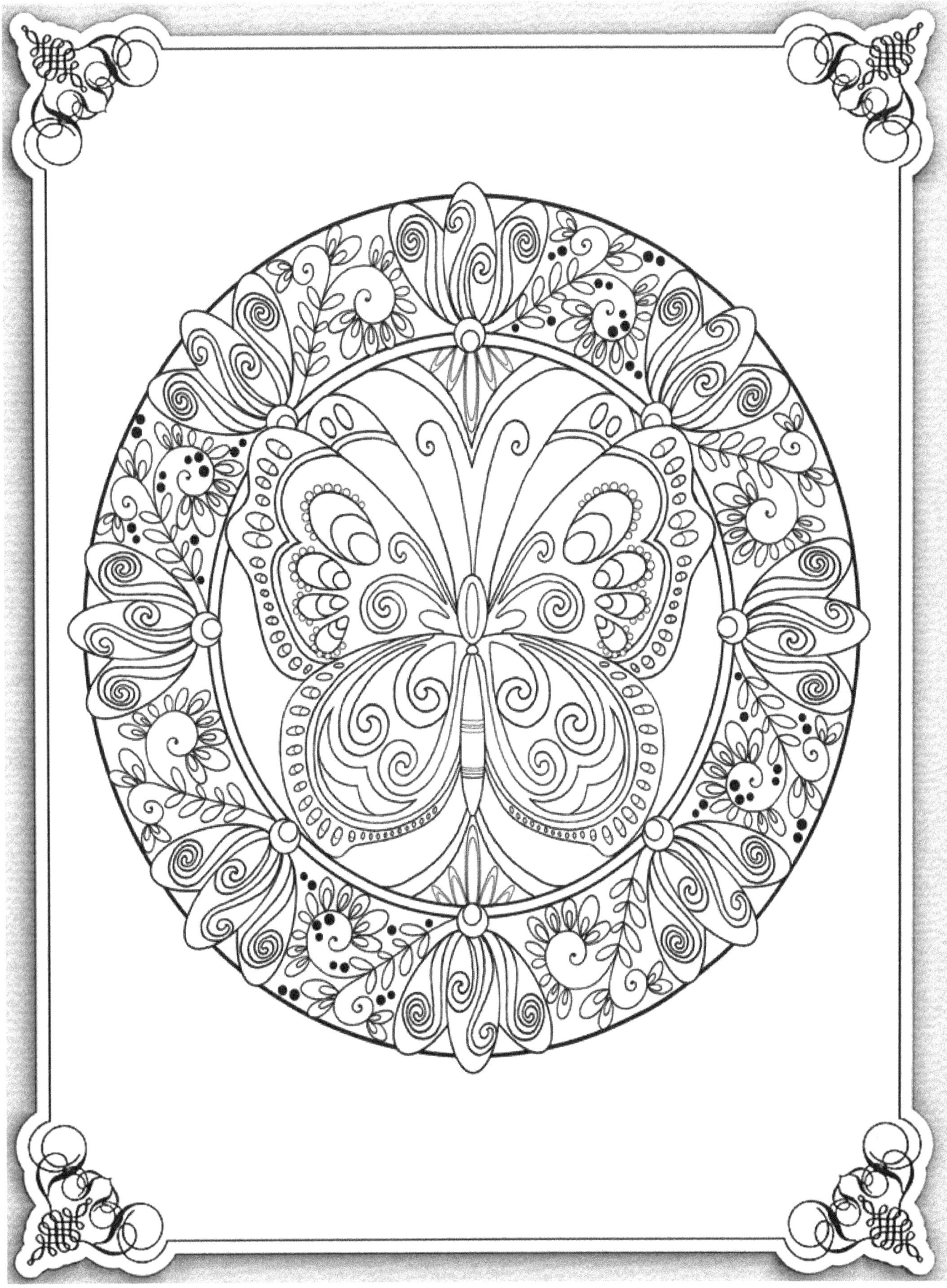

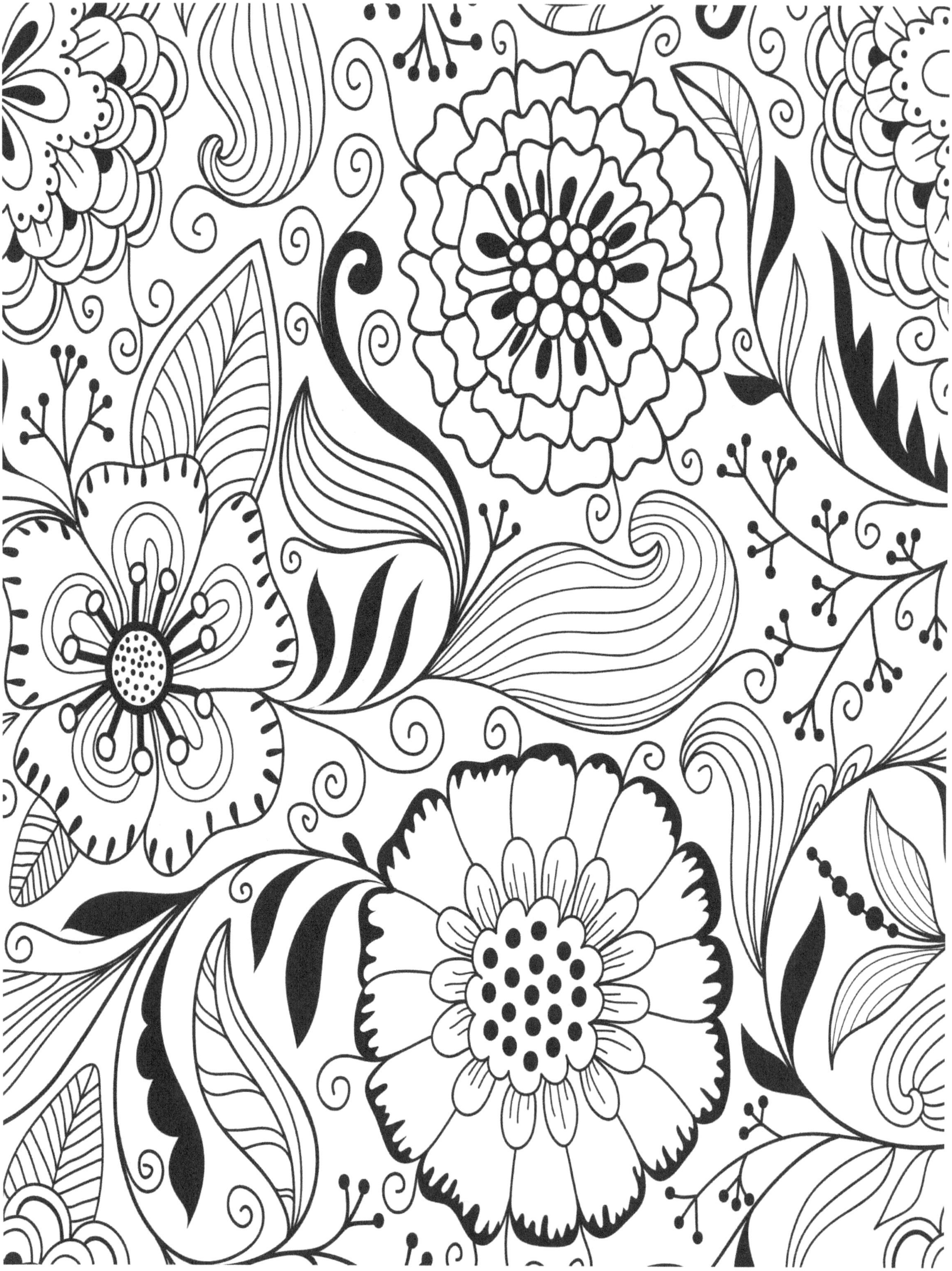

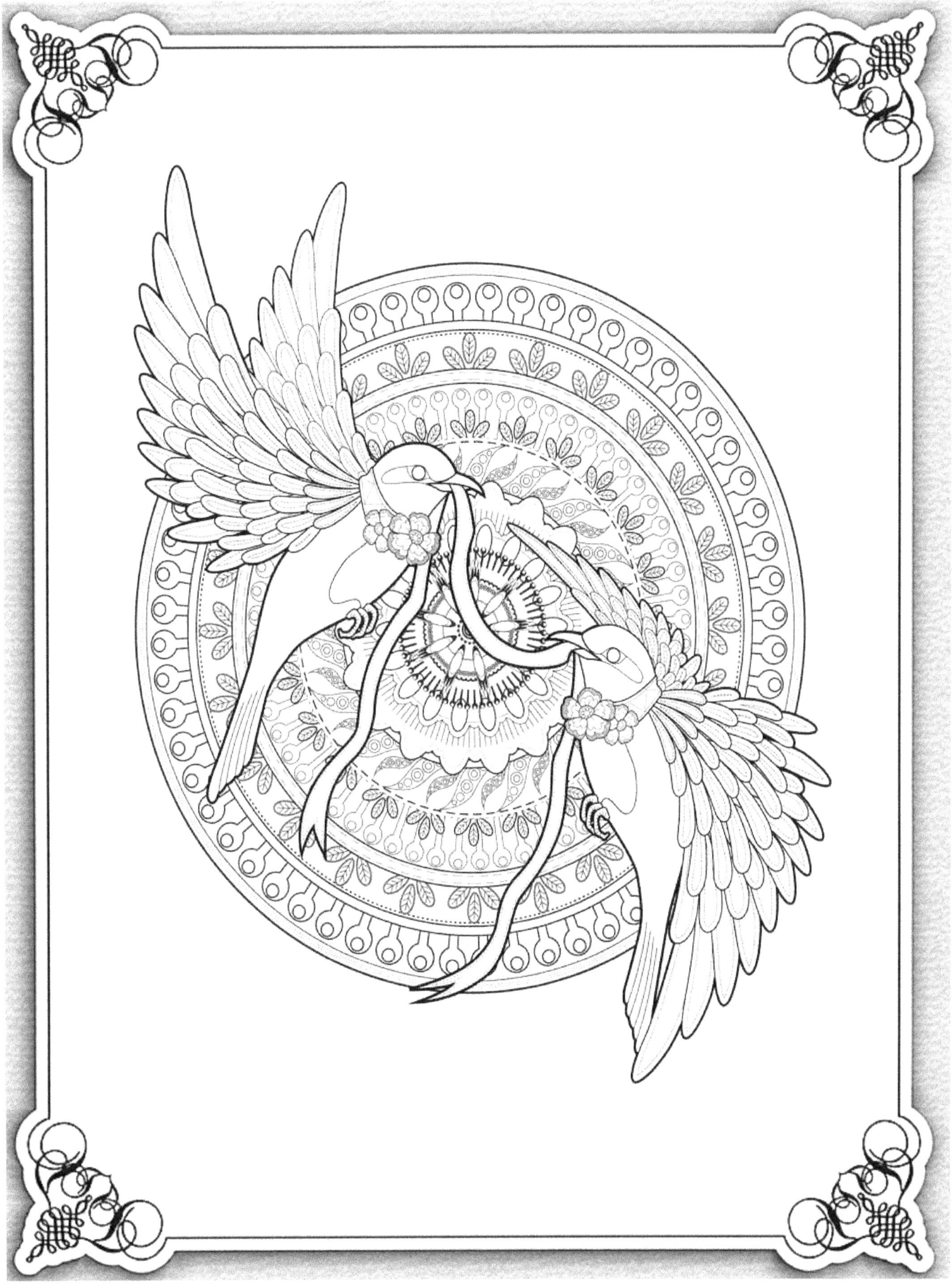

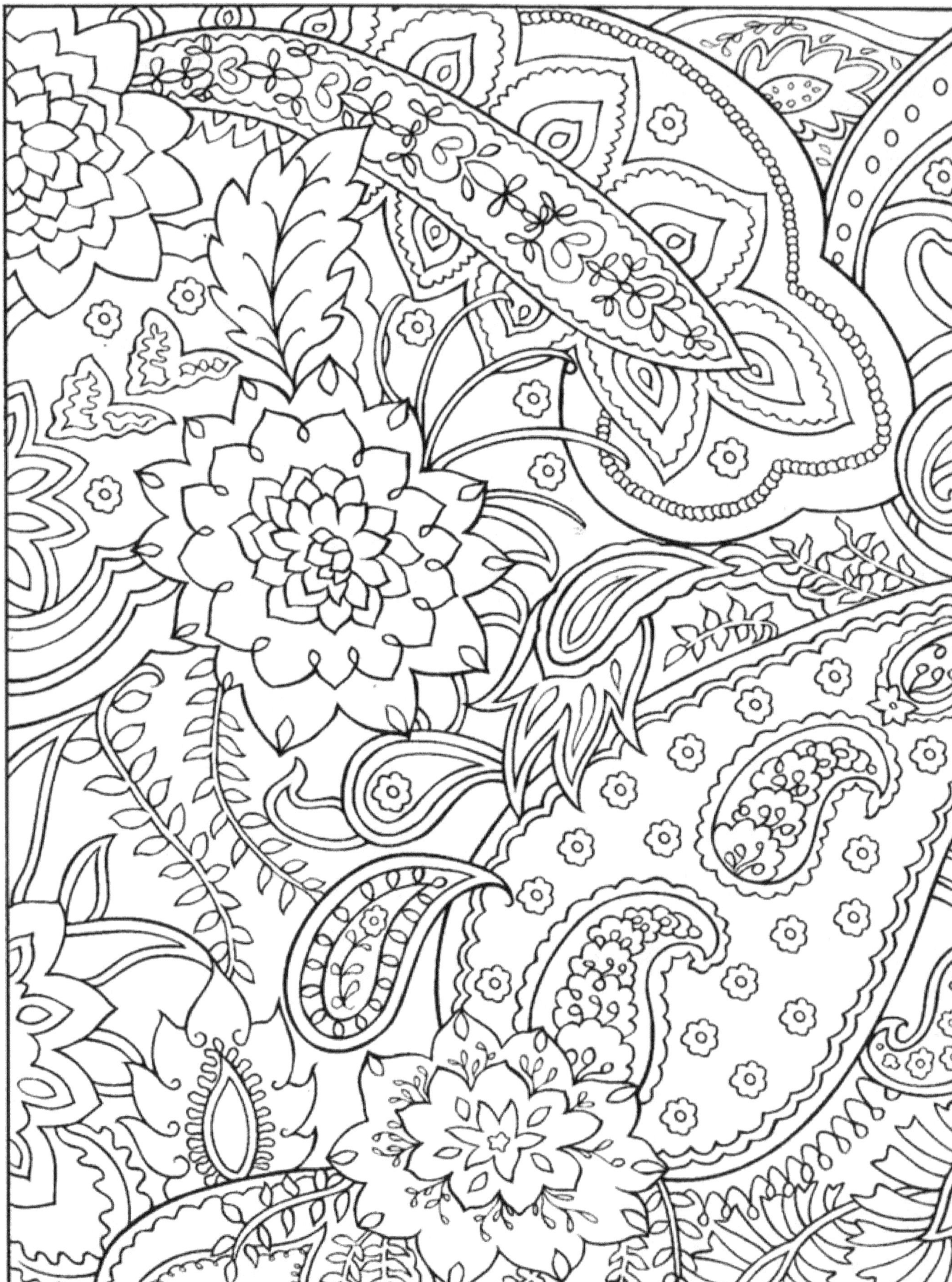

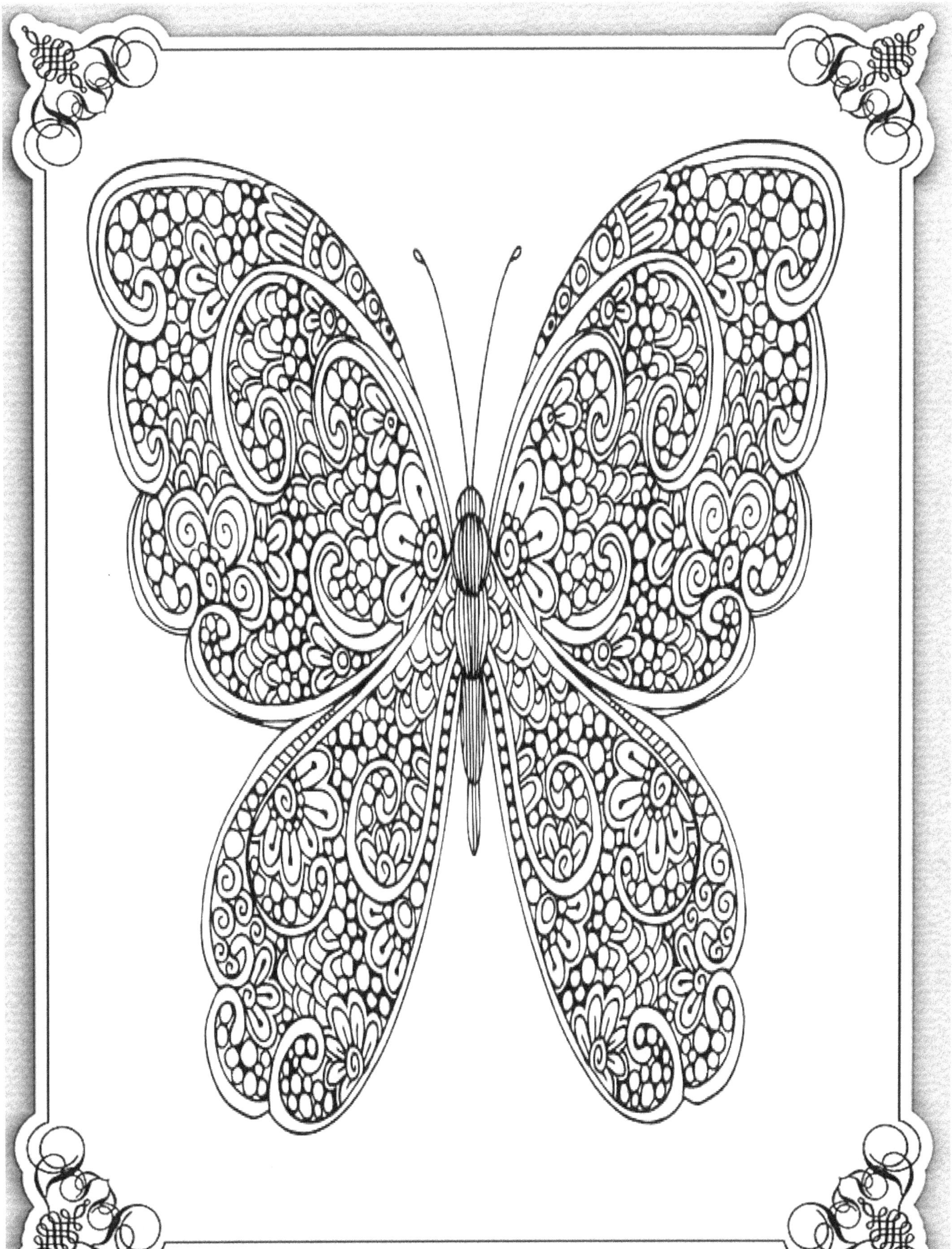

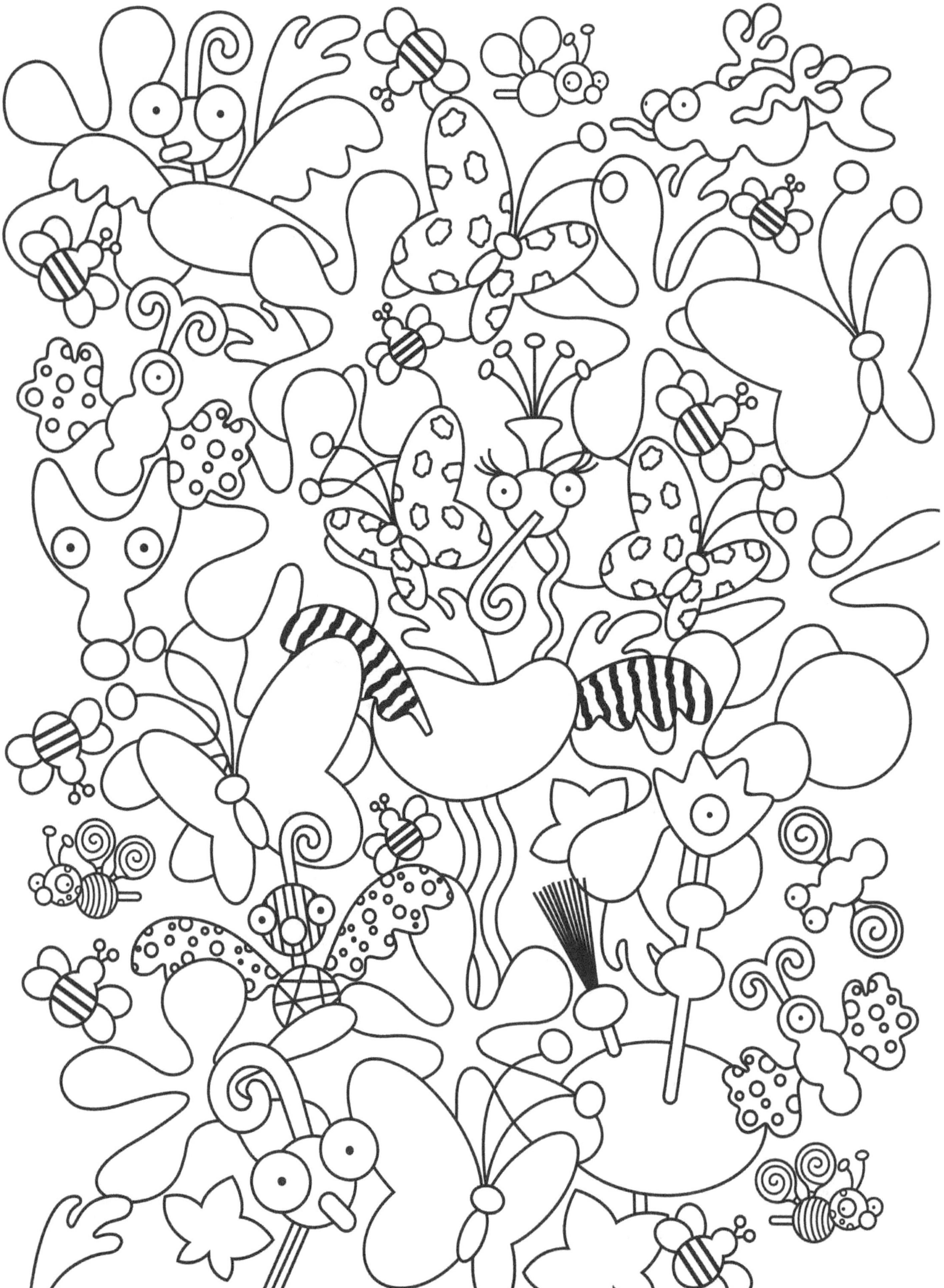

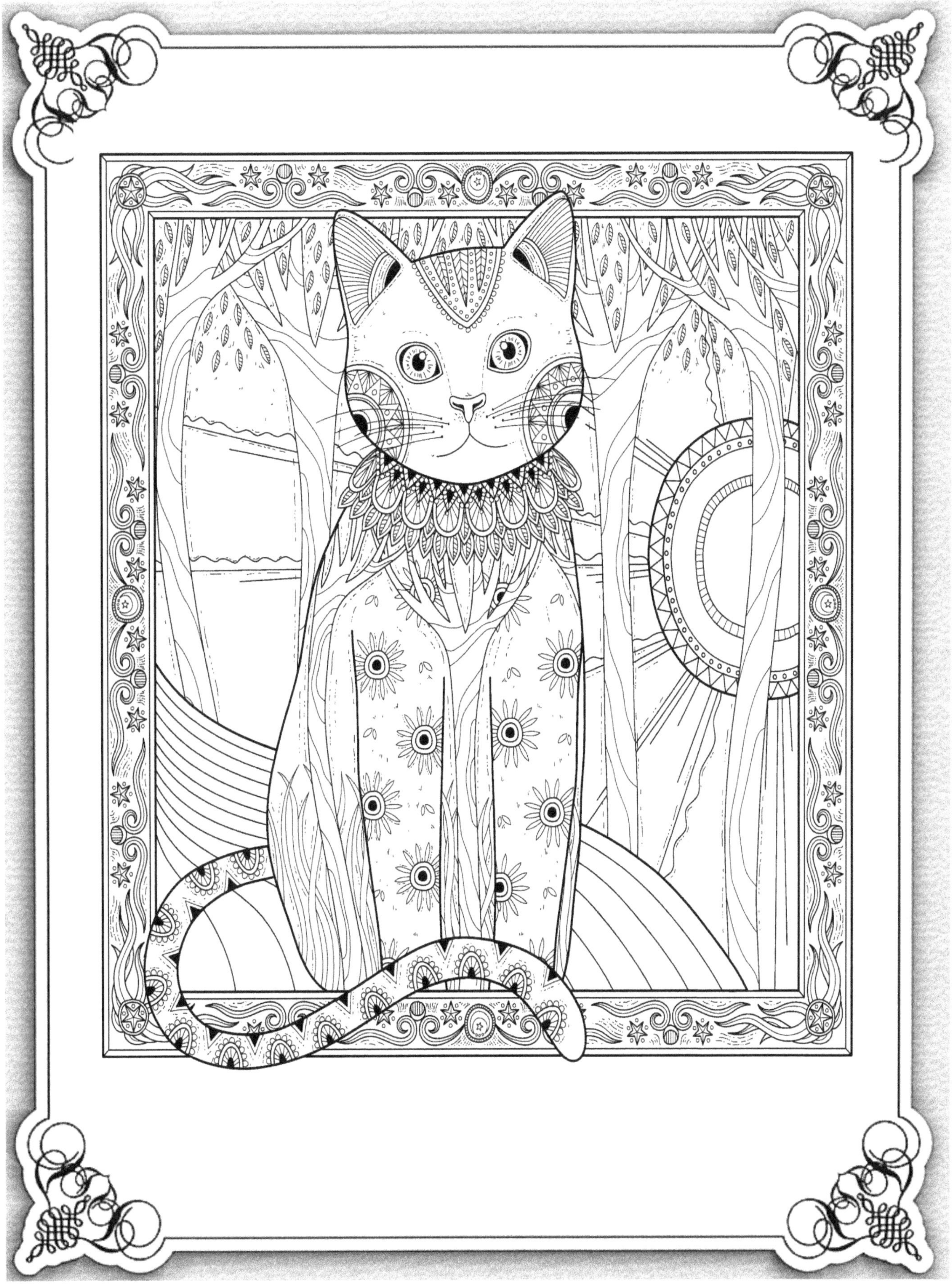

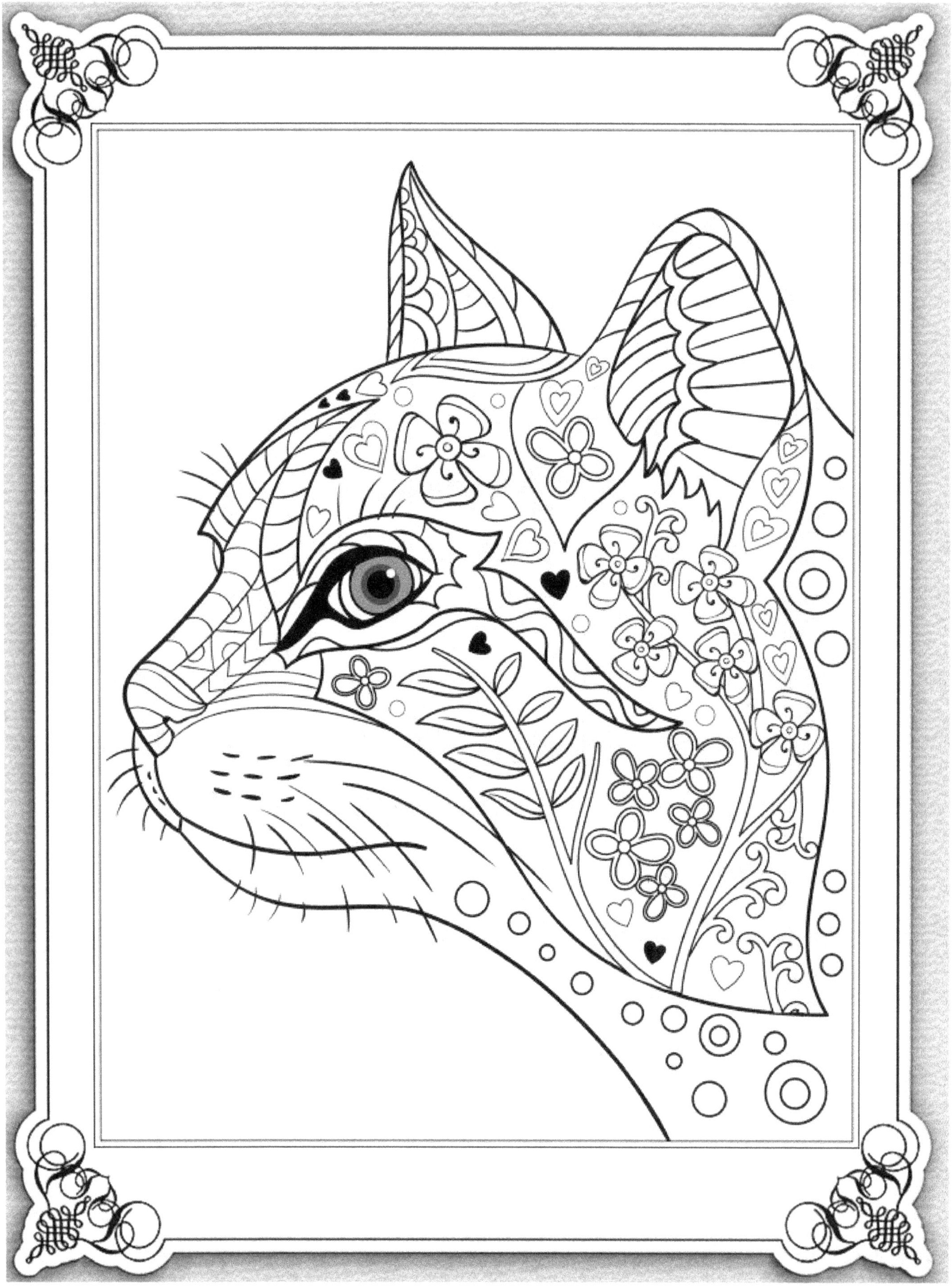

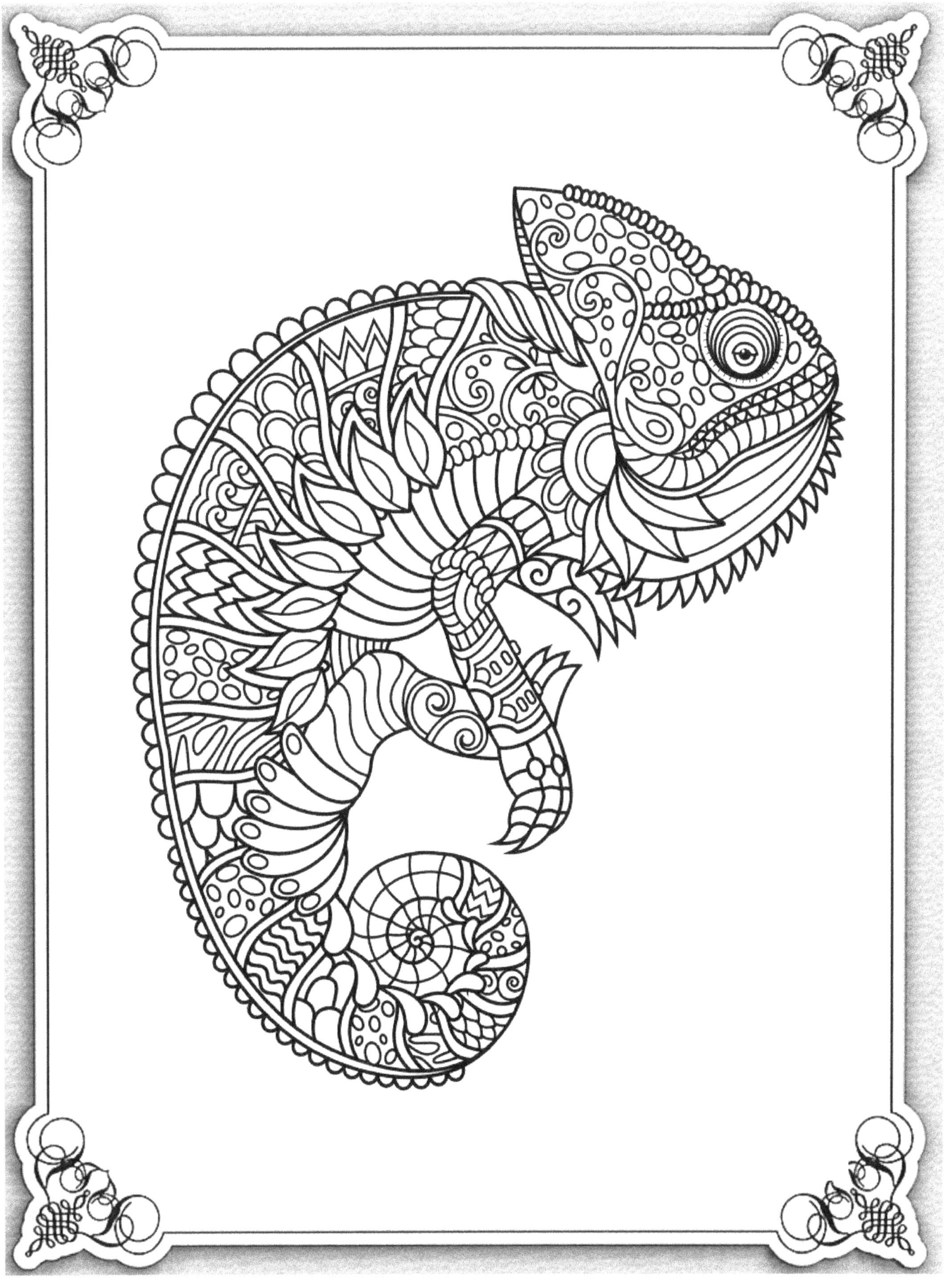

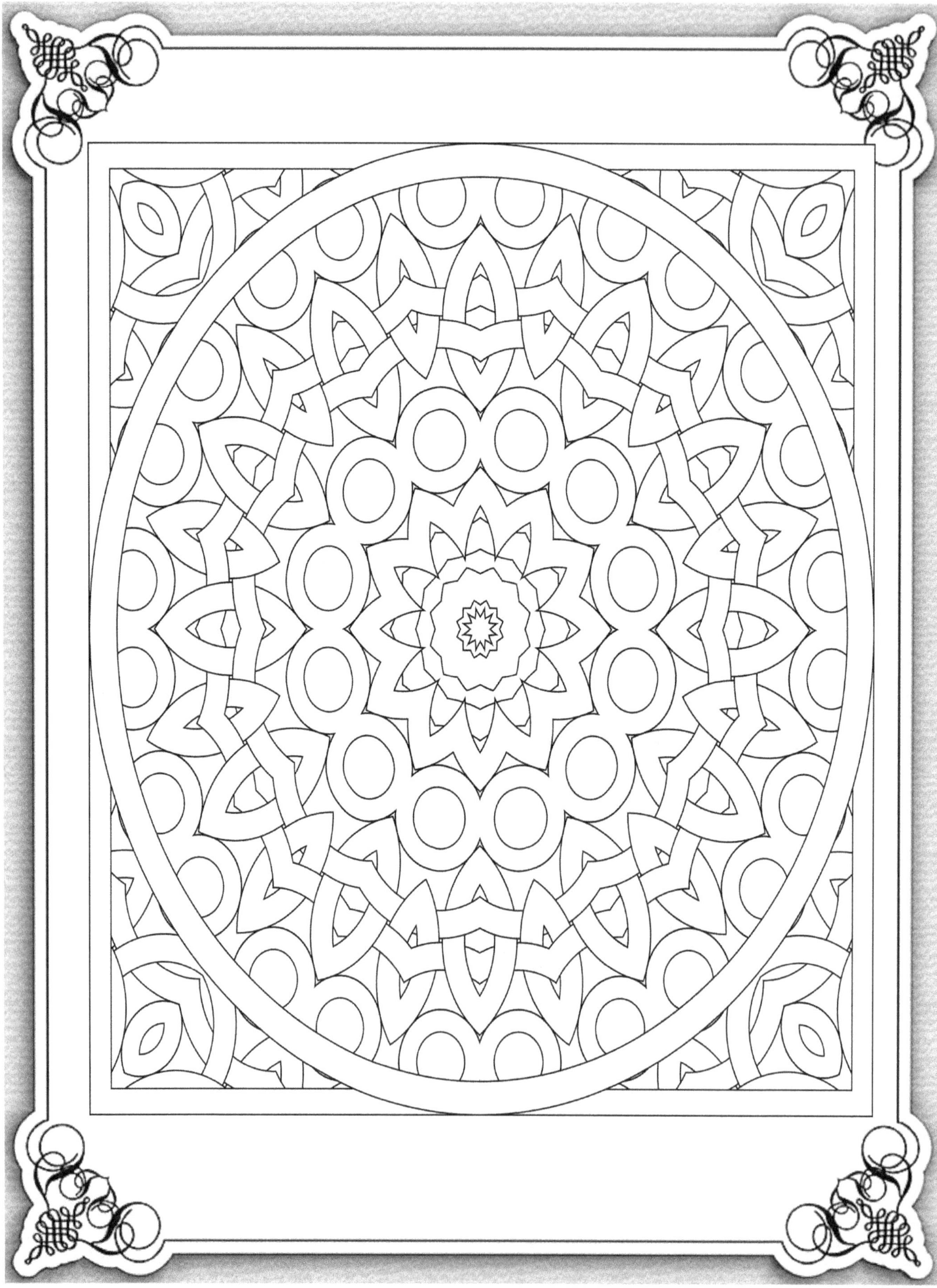

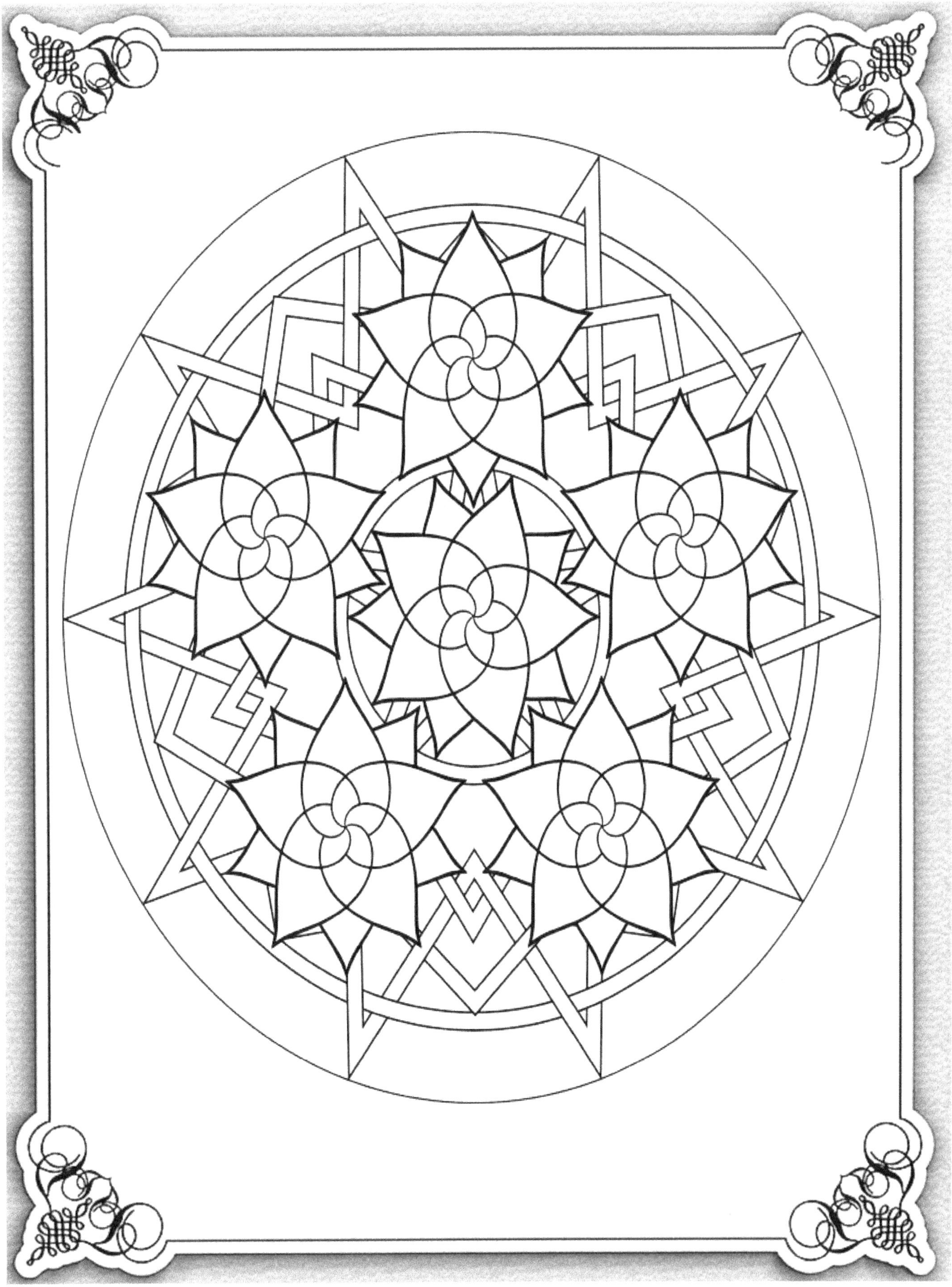

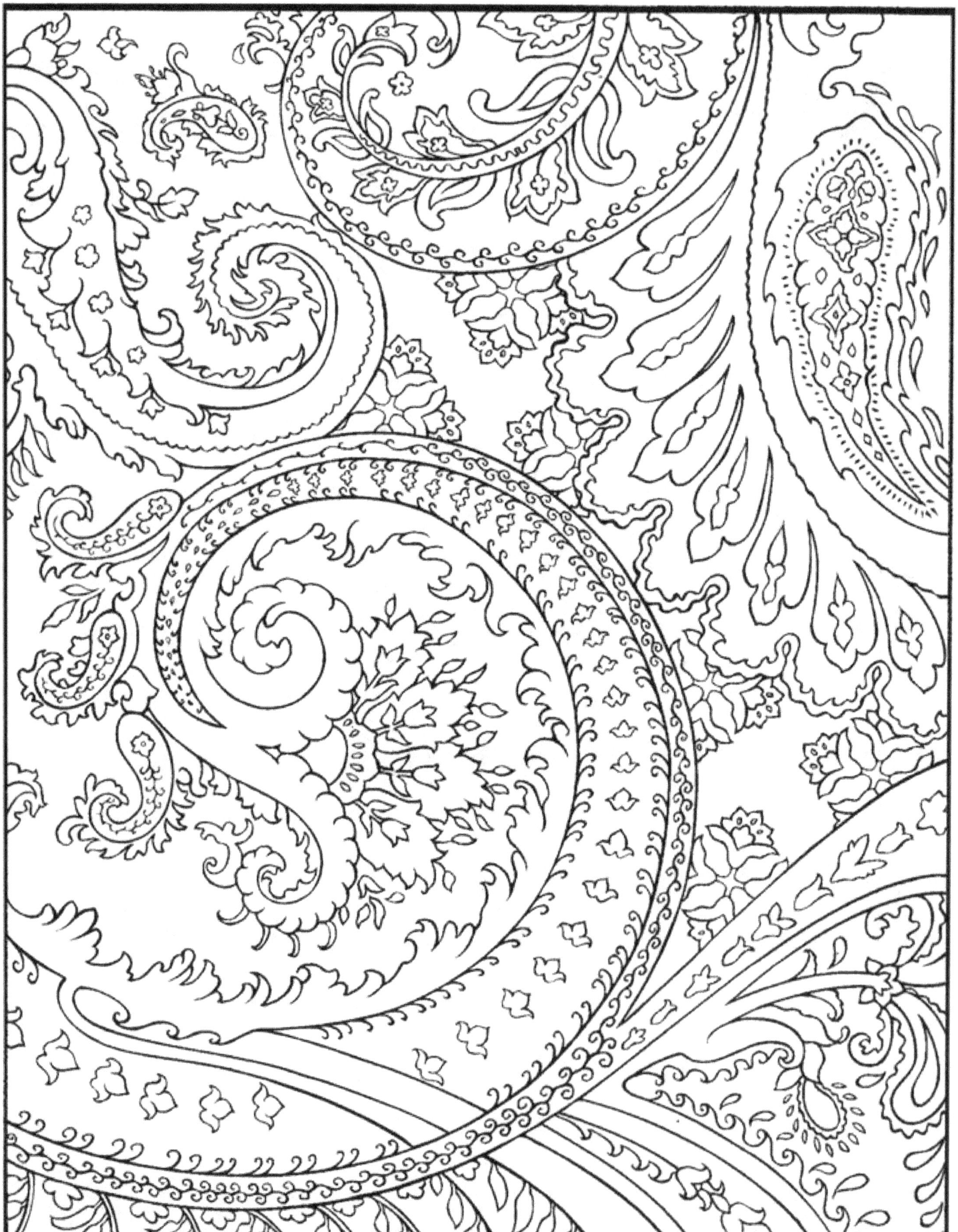

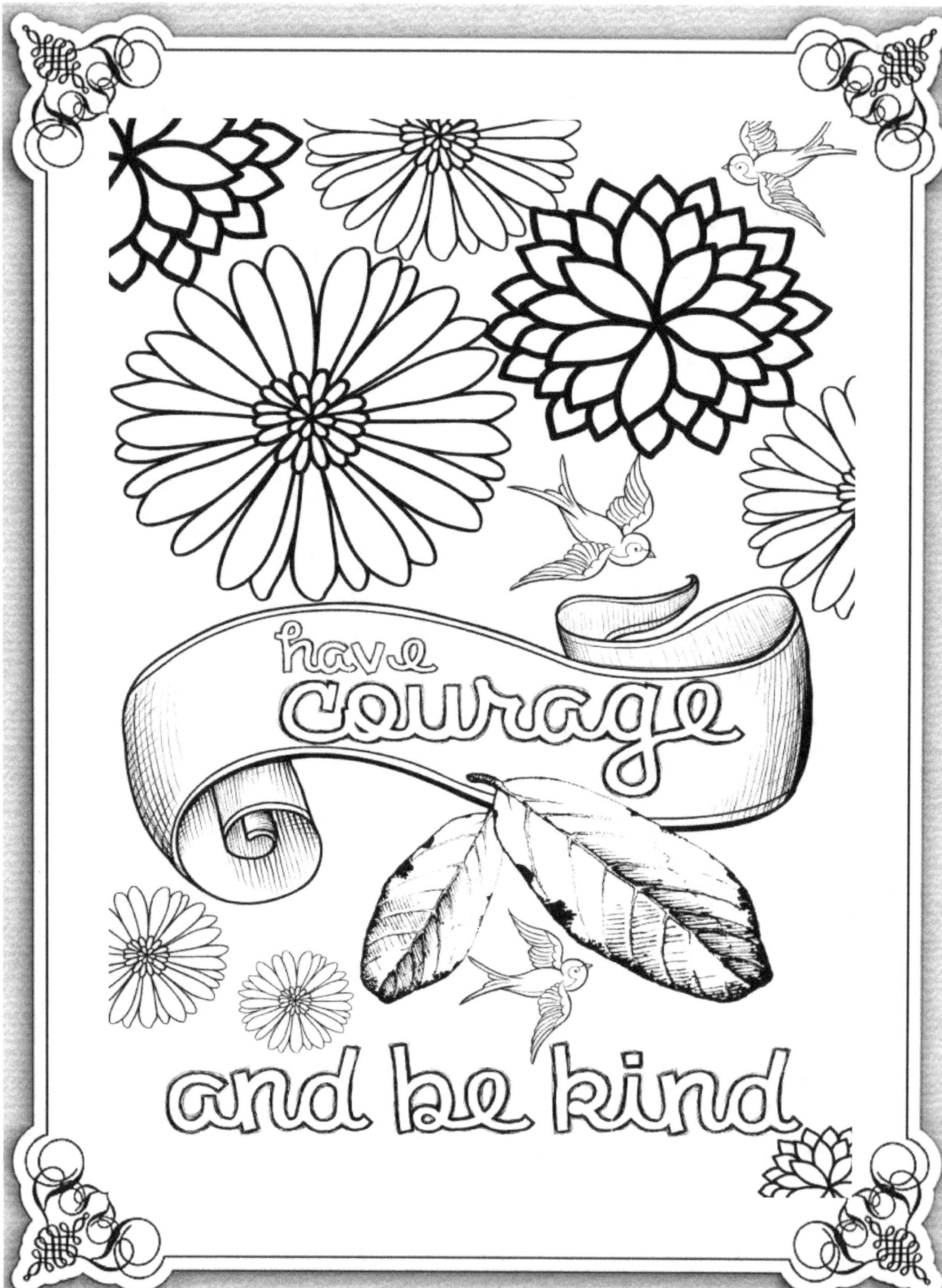
have
courage
and be kind

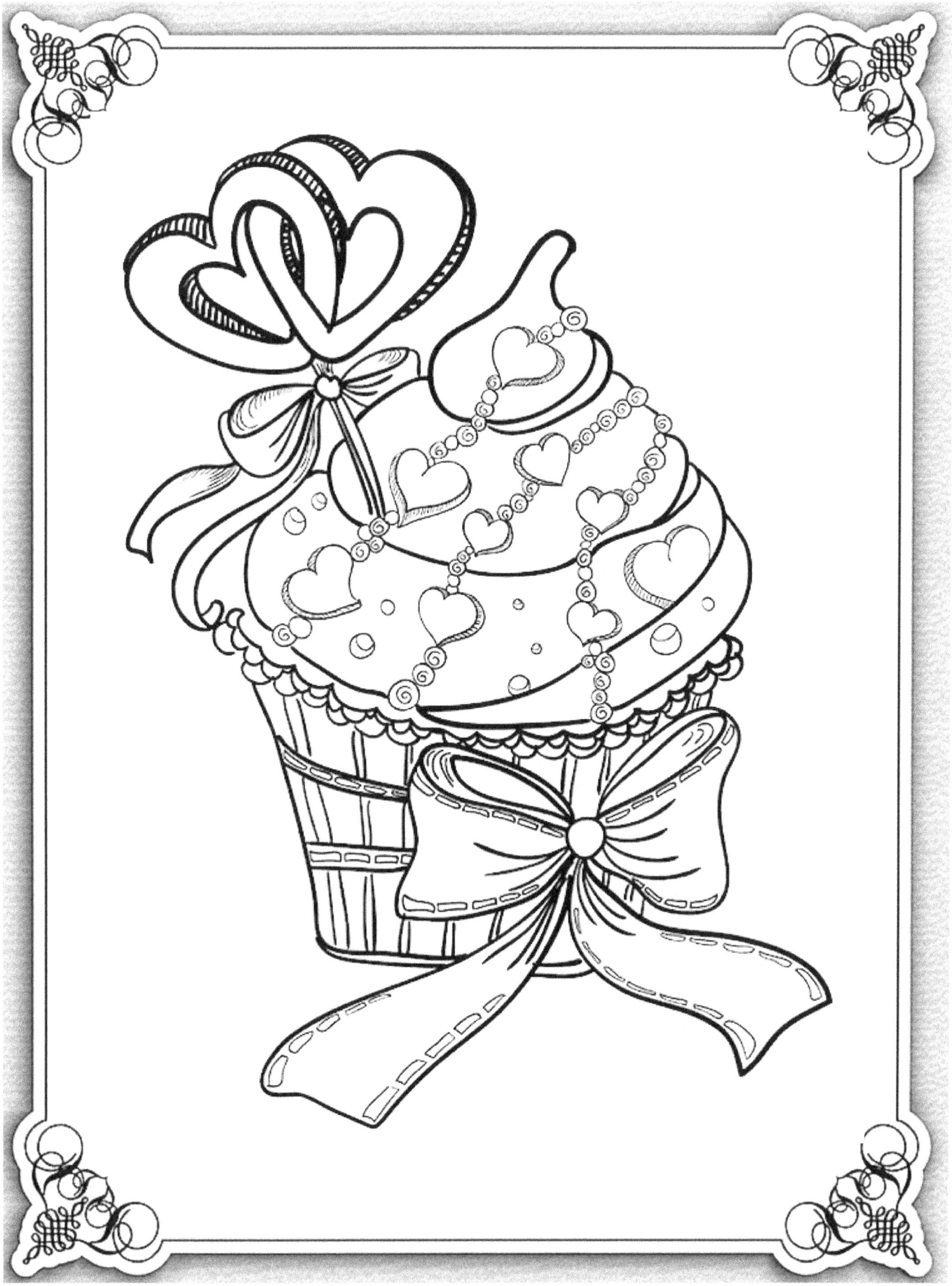

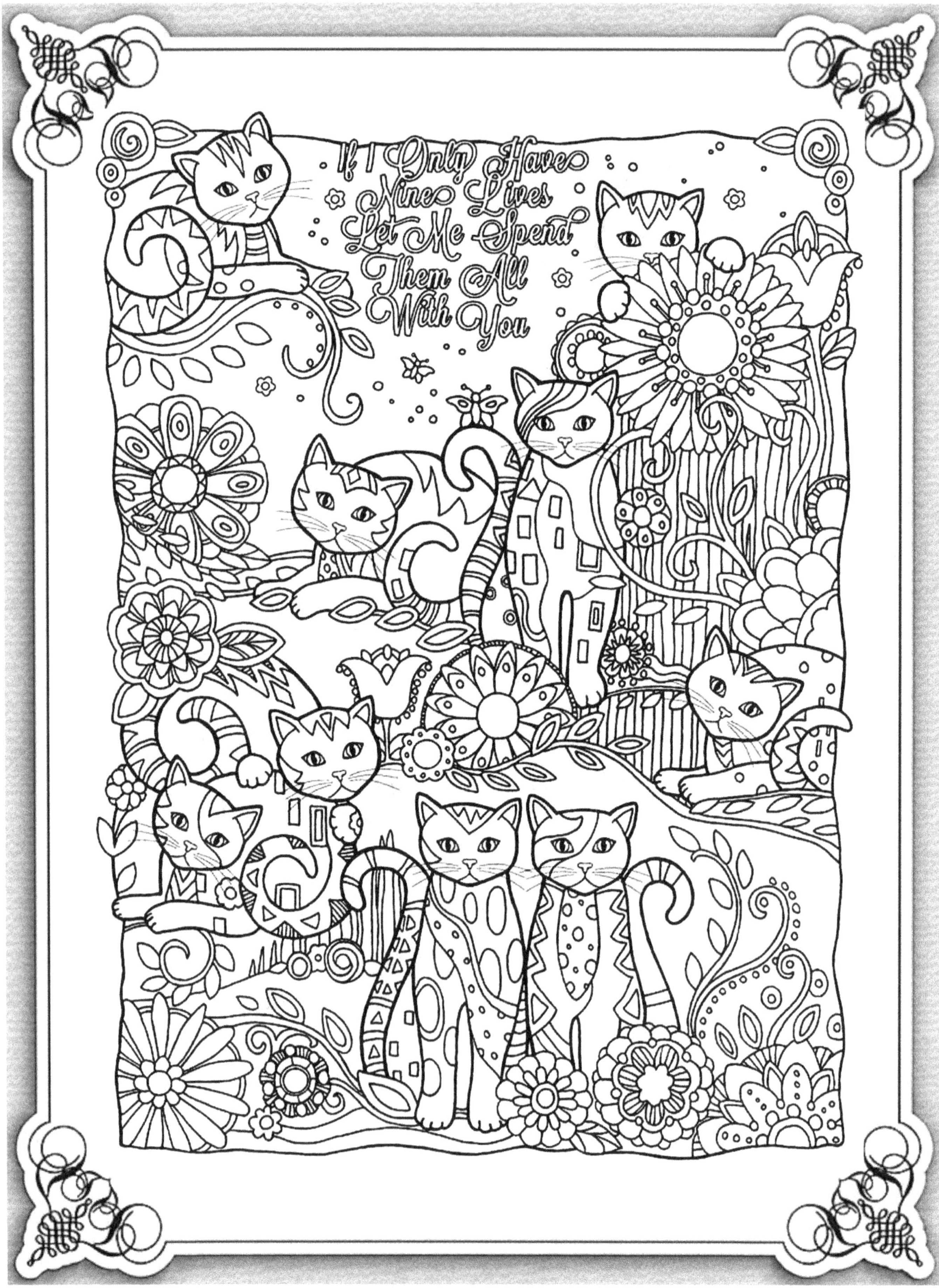
If I Only Have
Nine Lives
Let Me Spend
Them All
With You

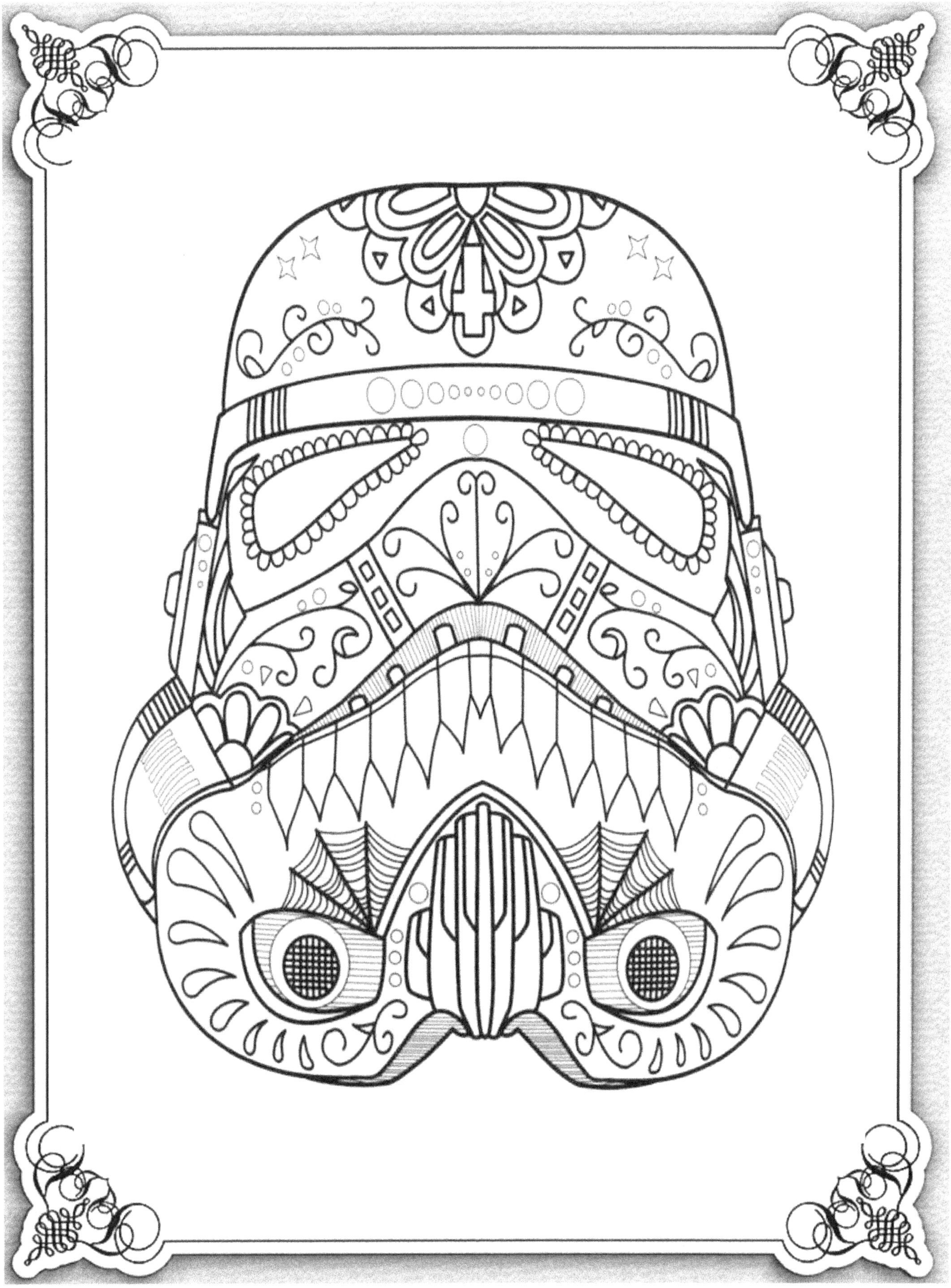

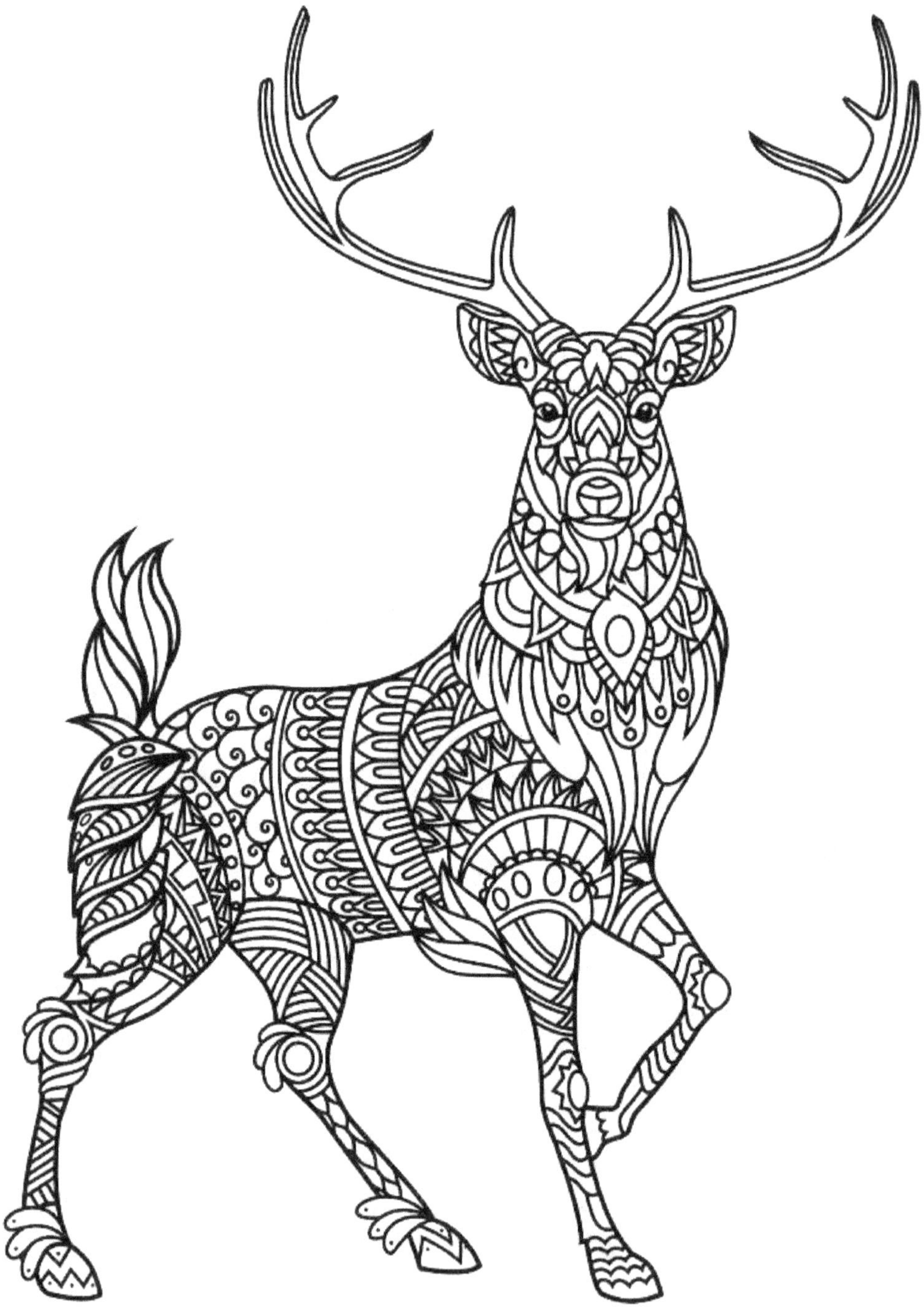

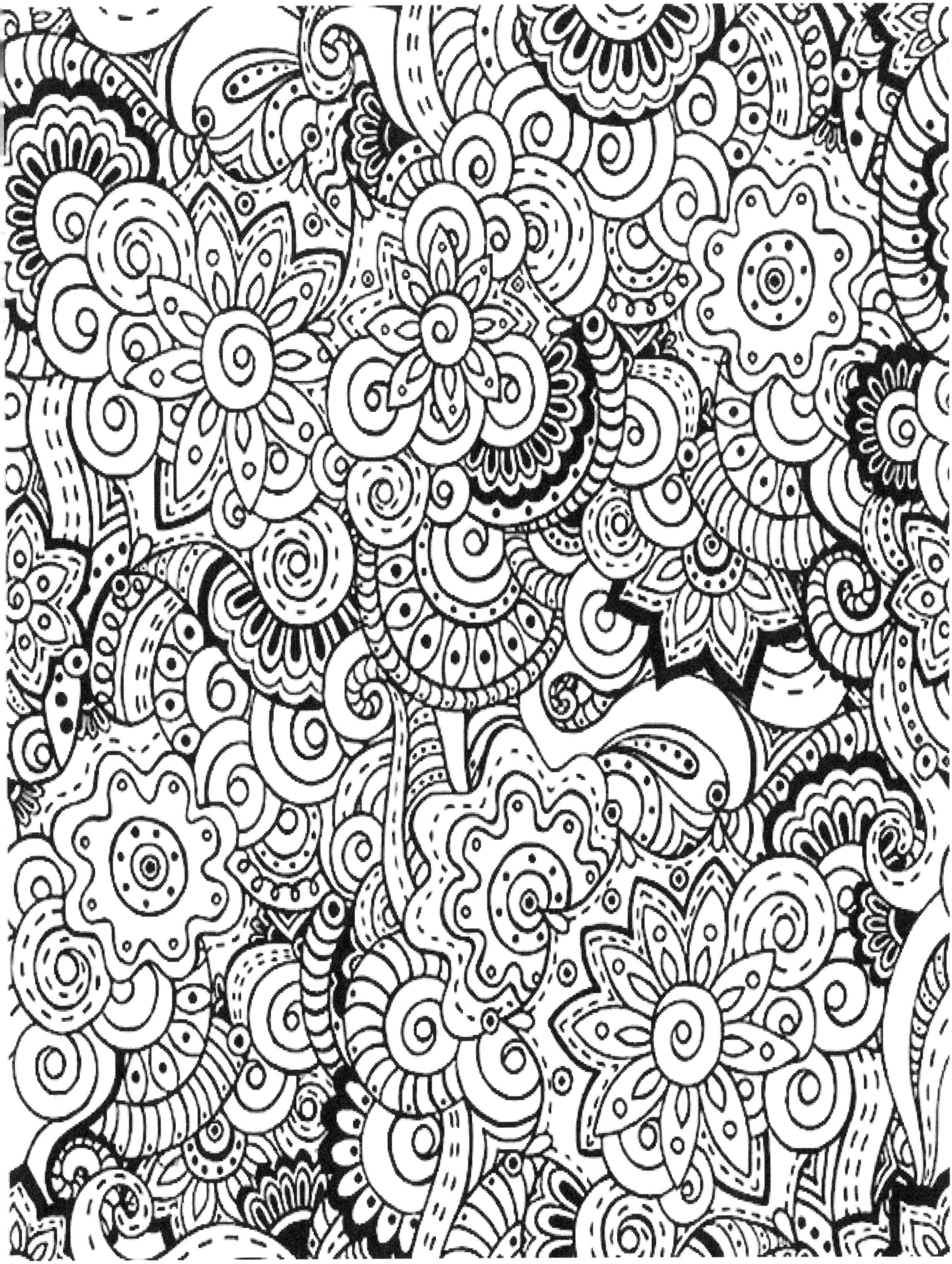

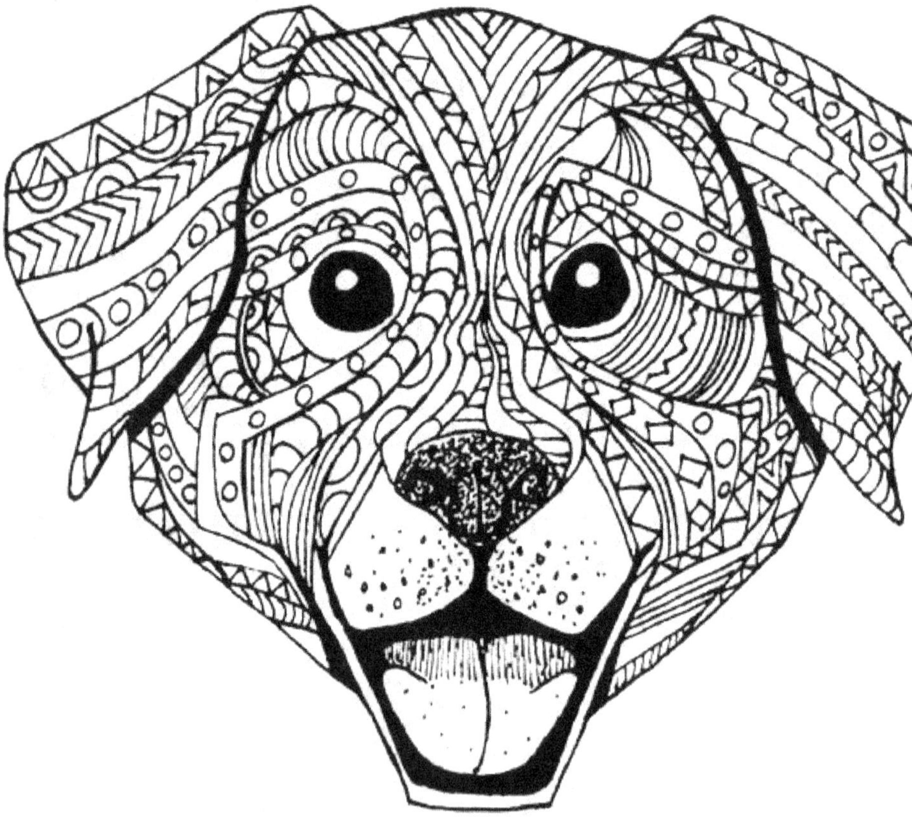

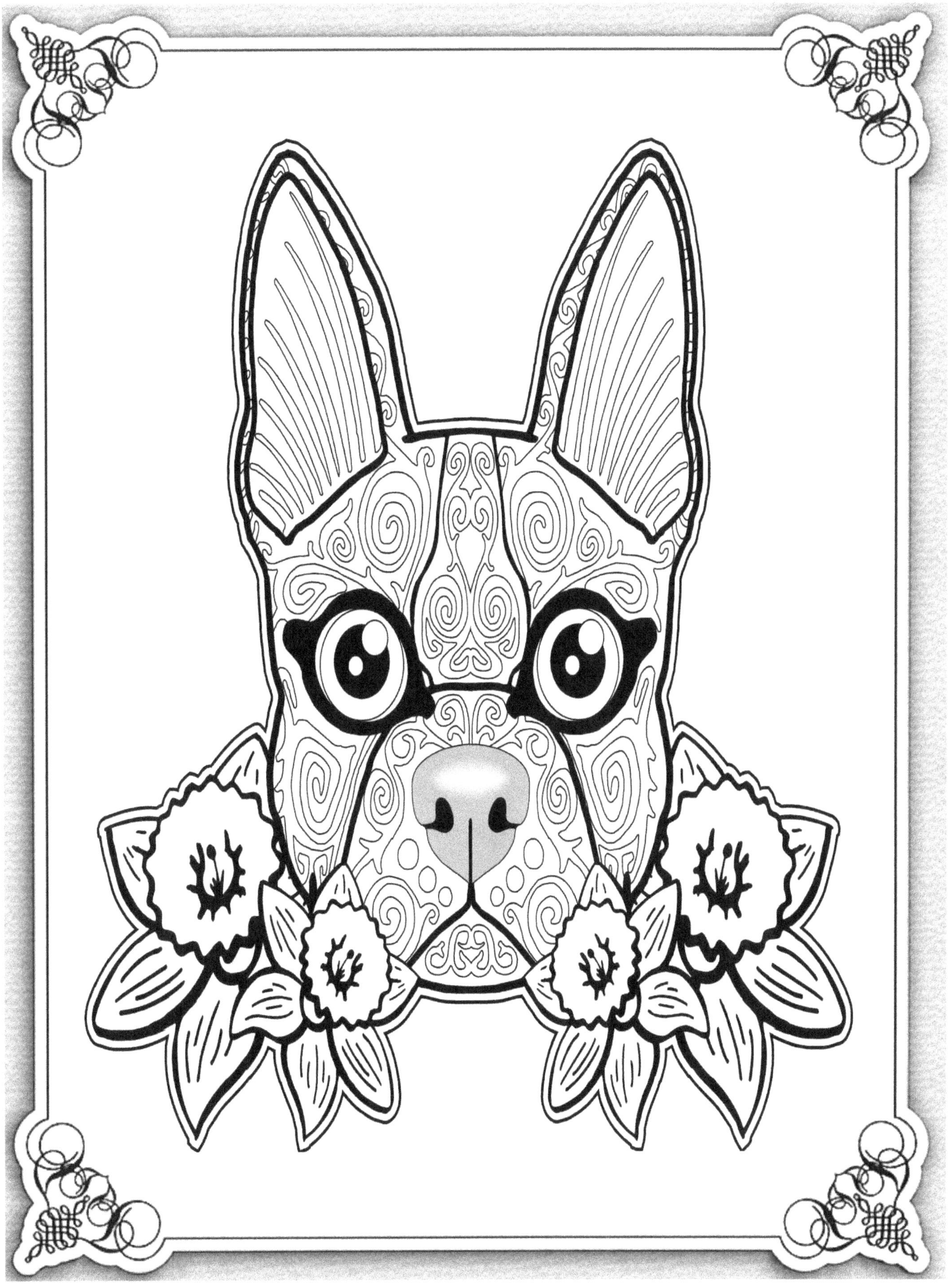

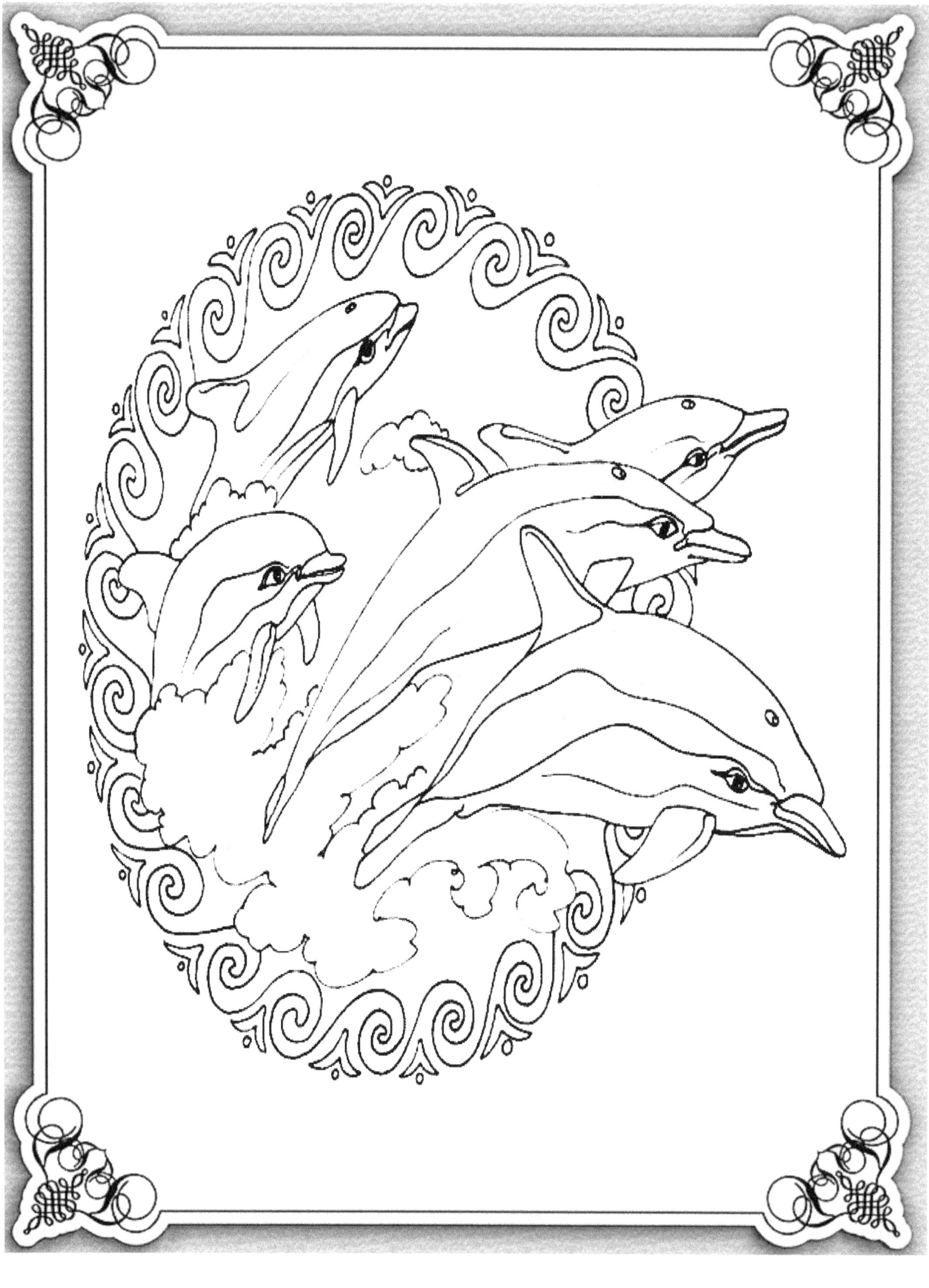

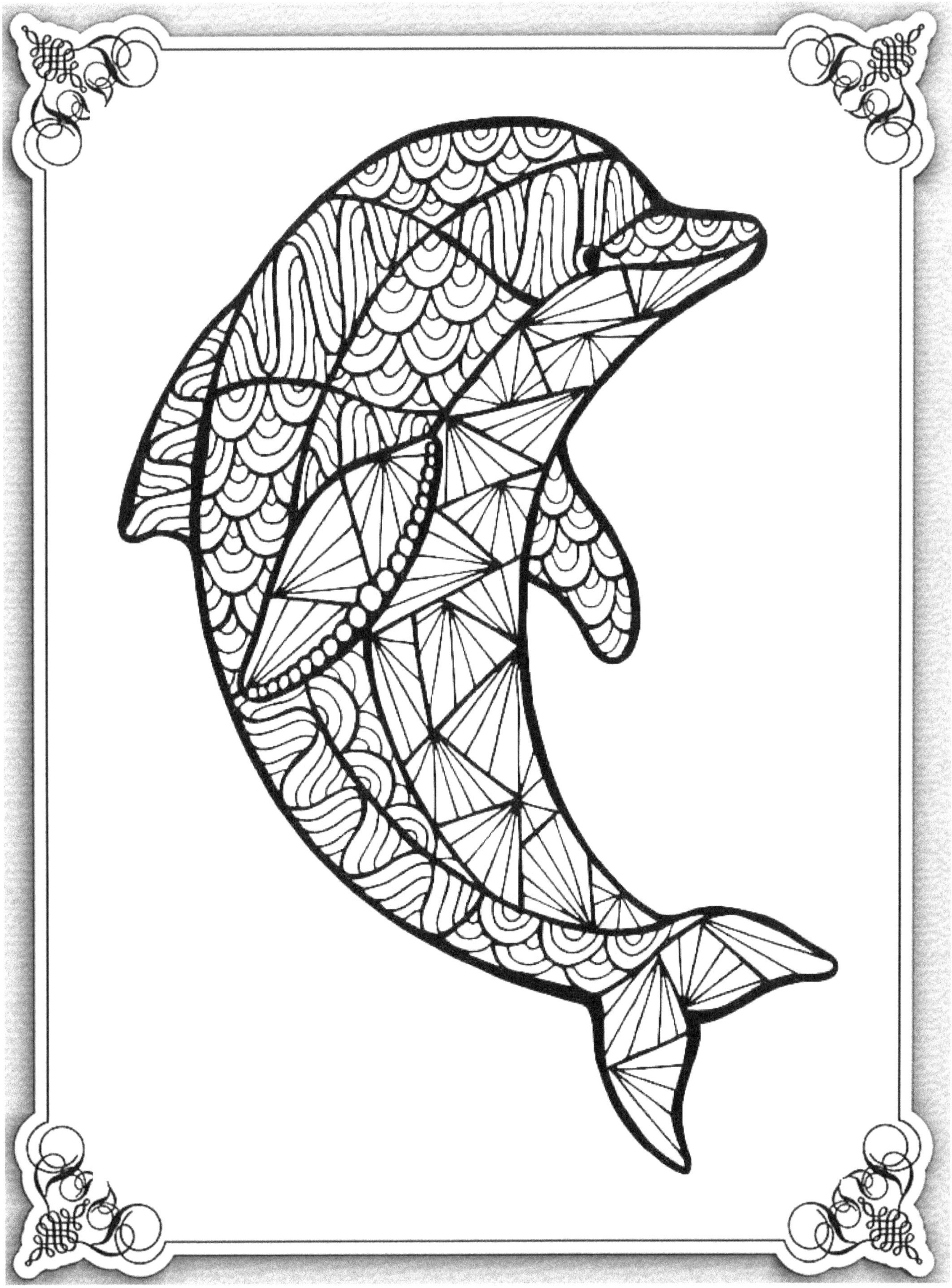

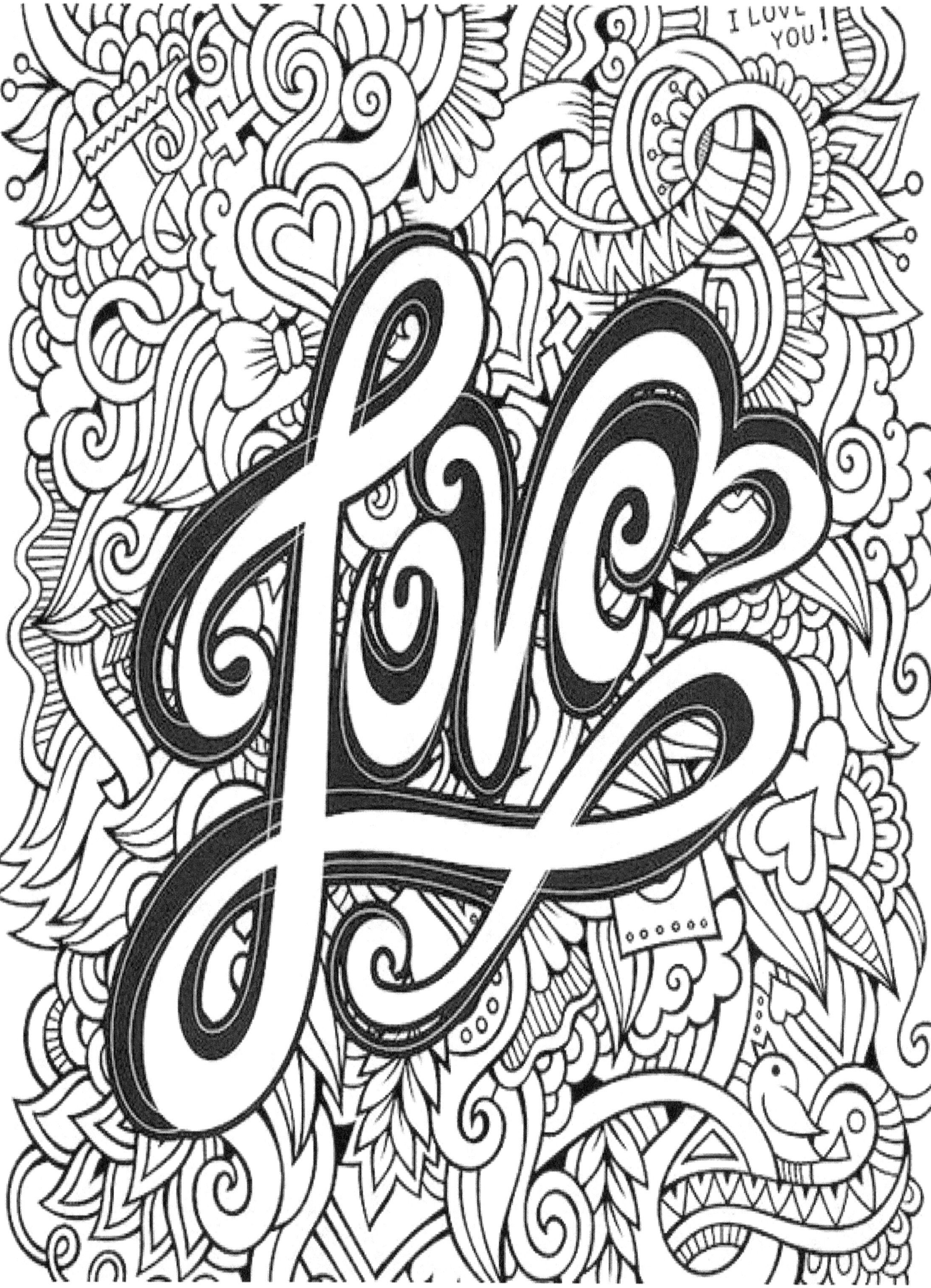
I LOVE YOU!
Love

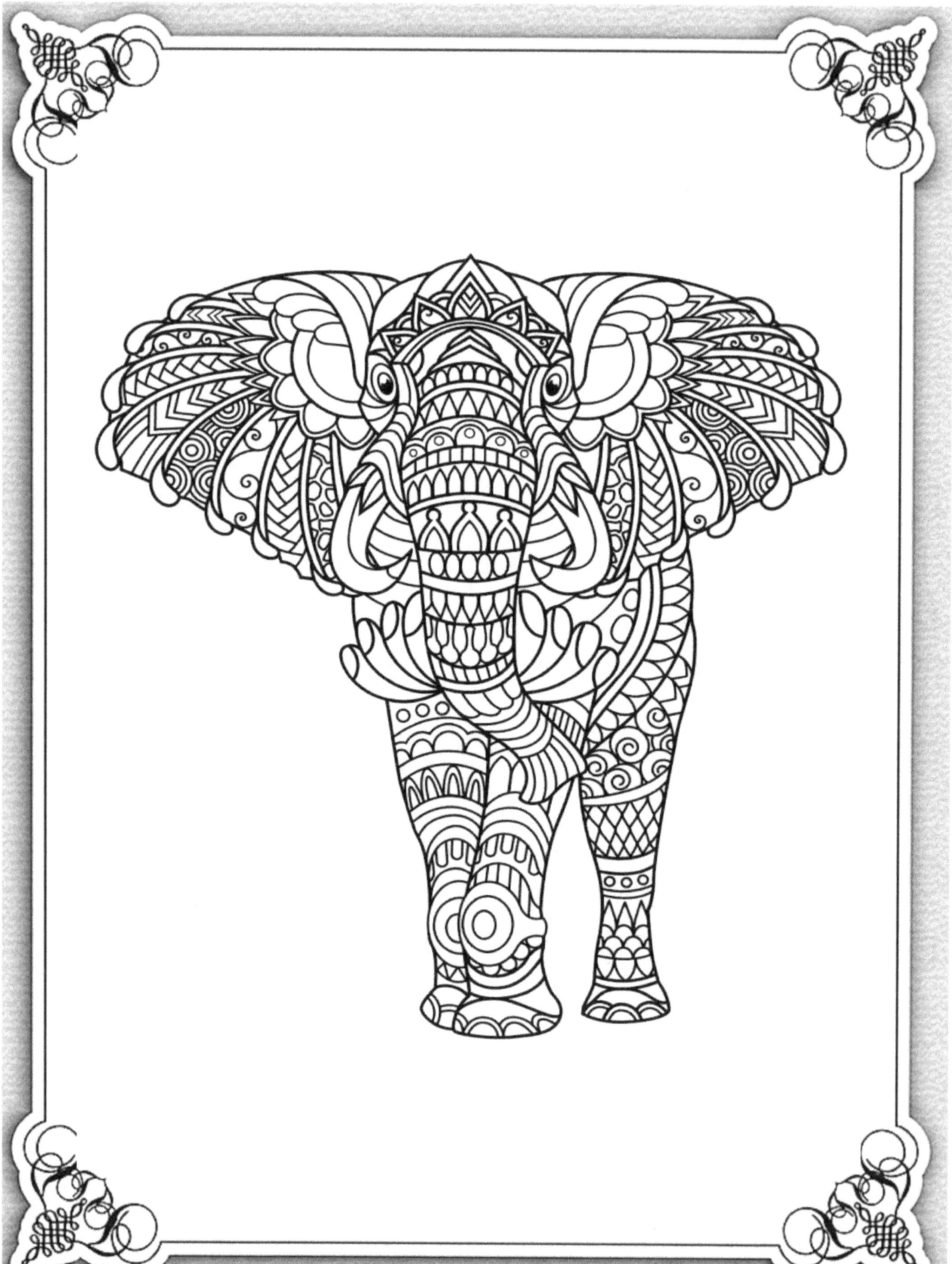

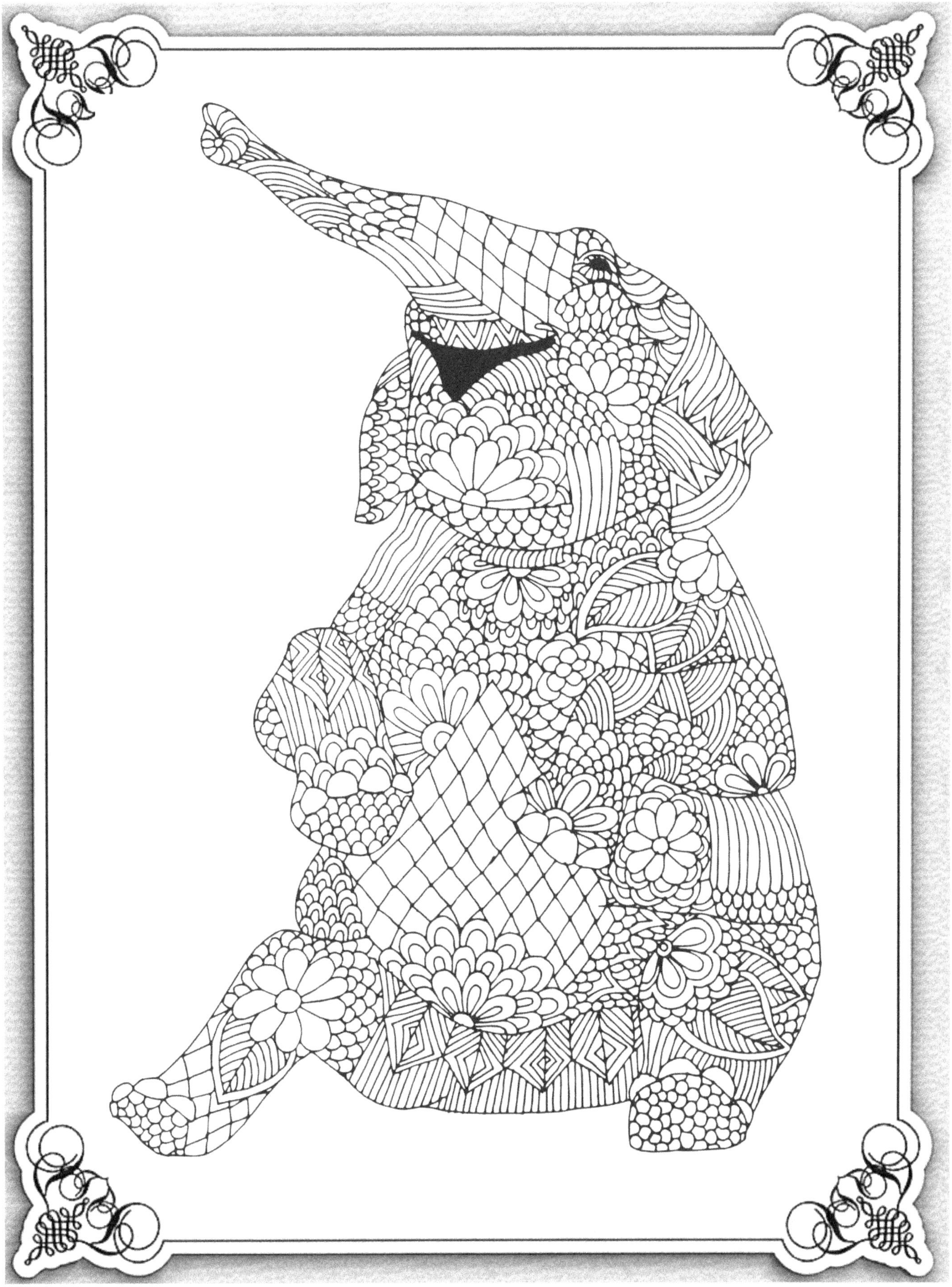

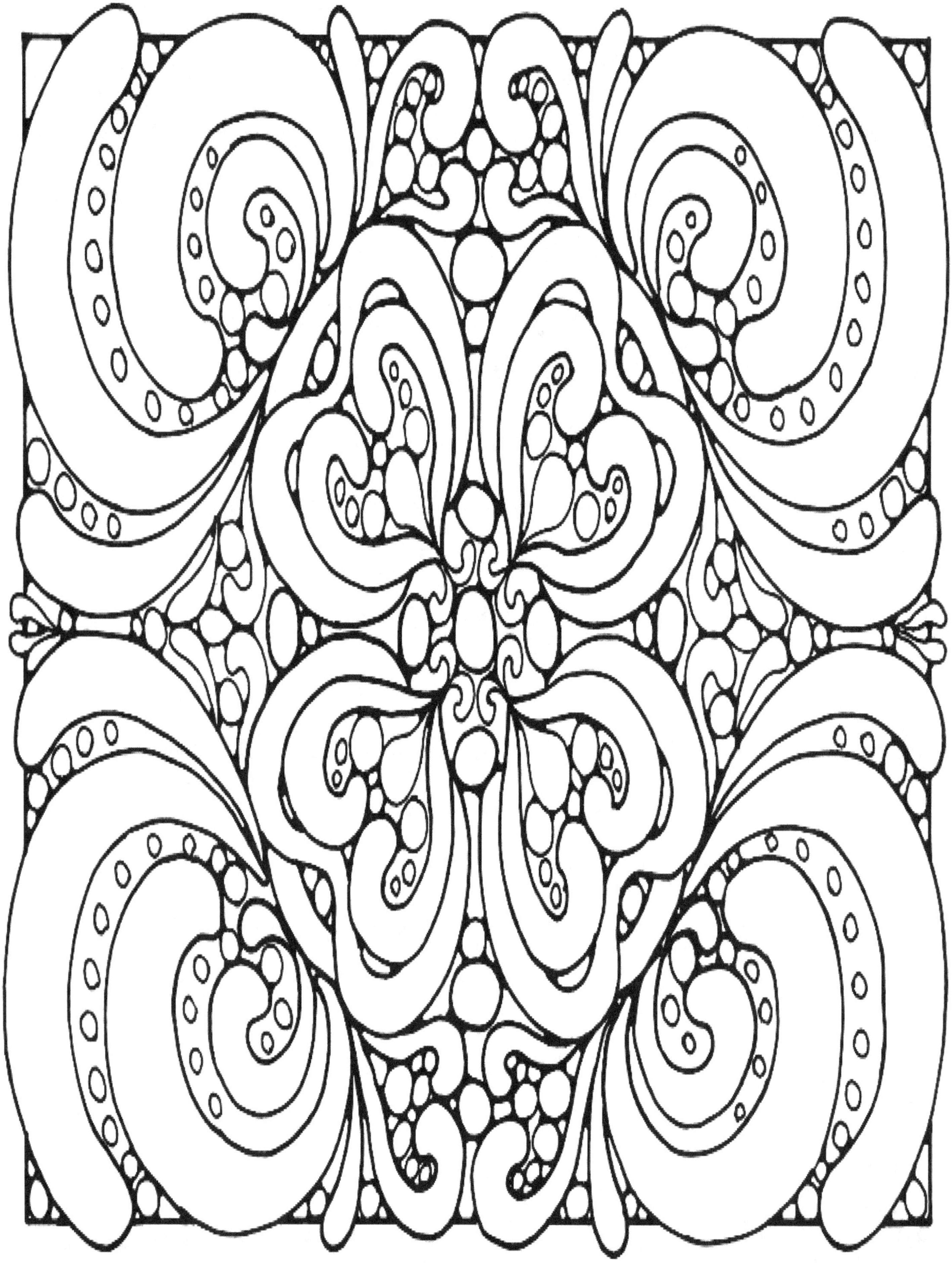

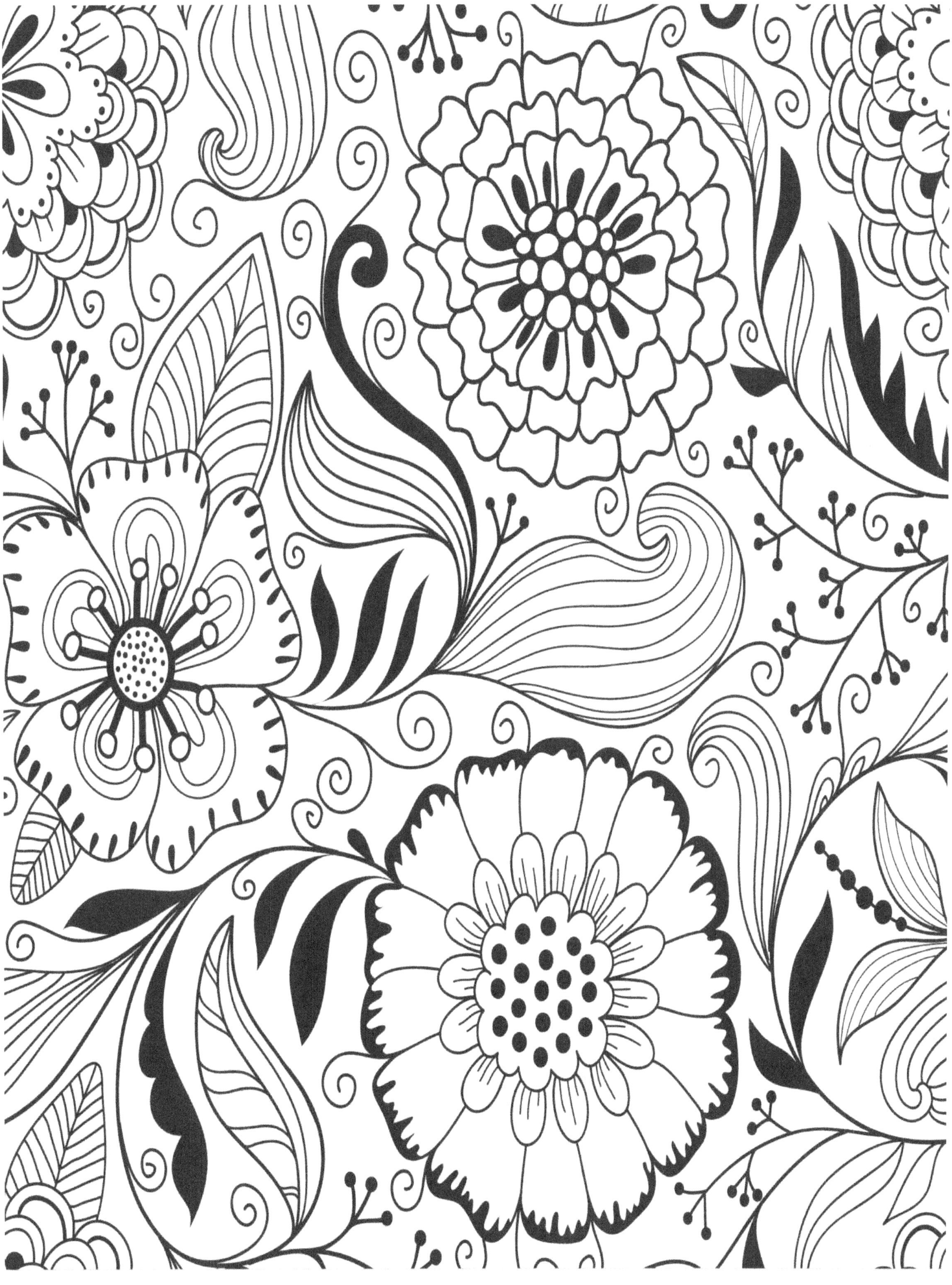

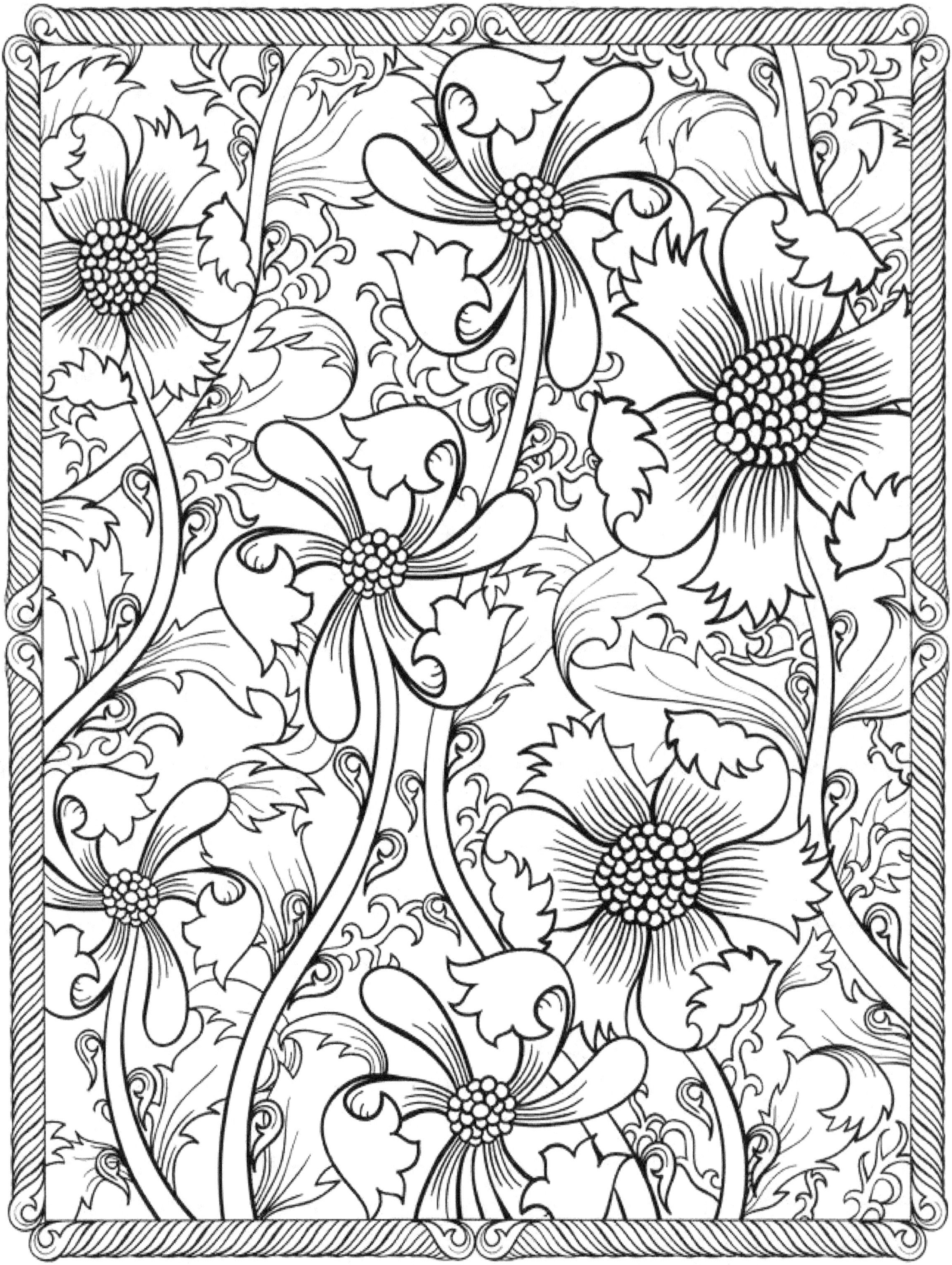

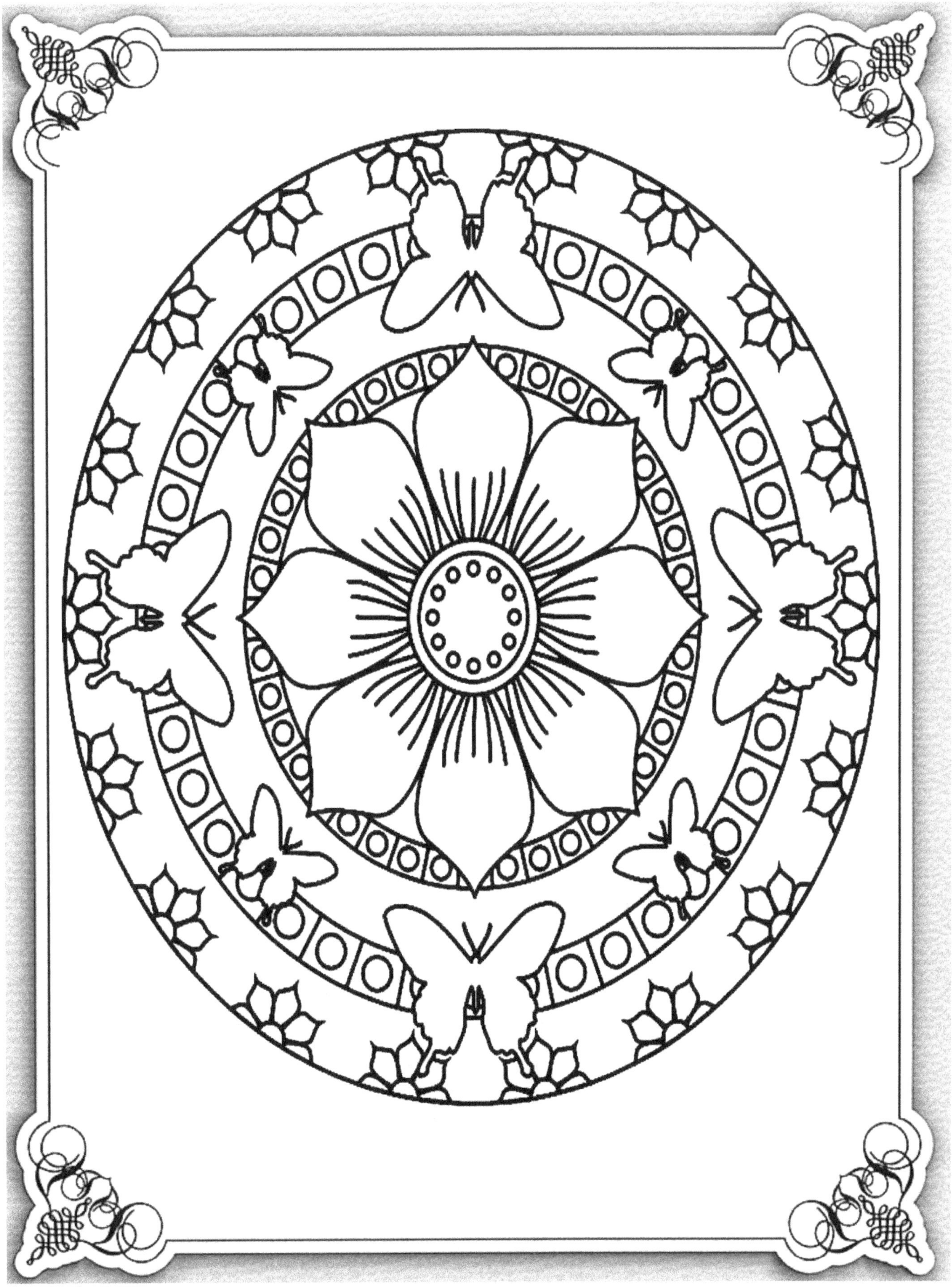

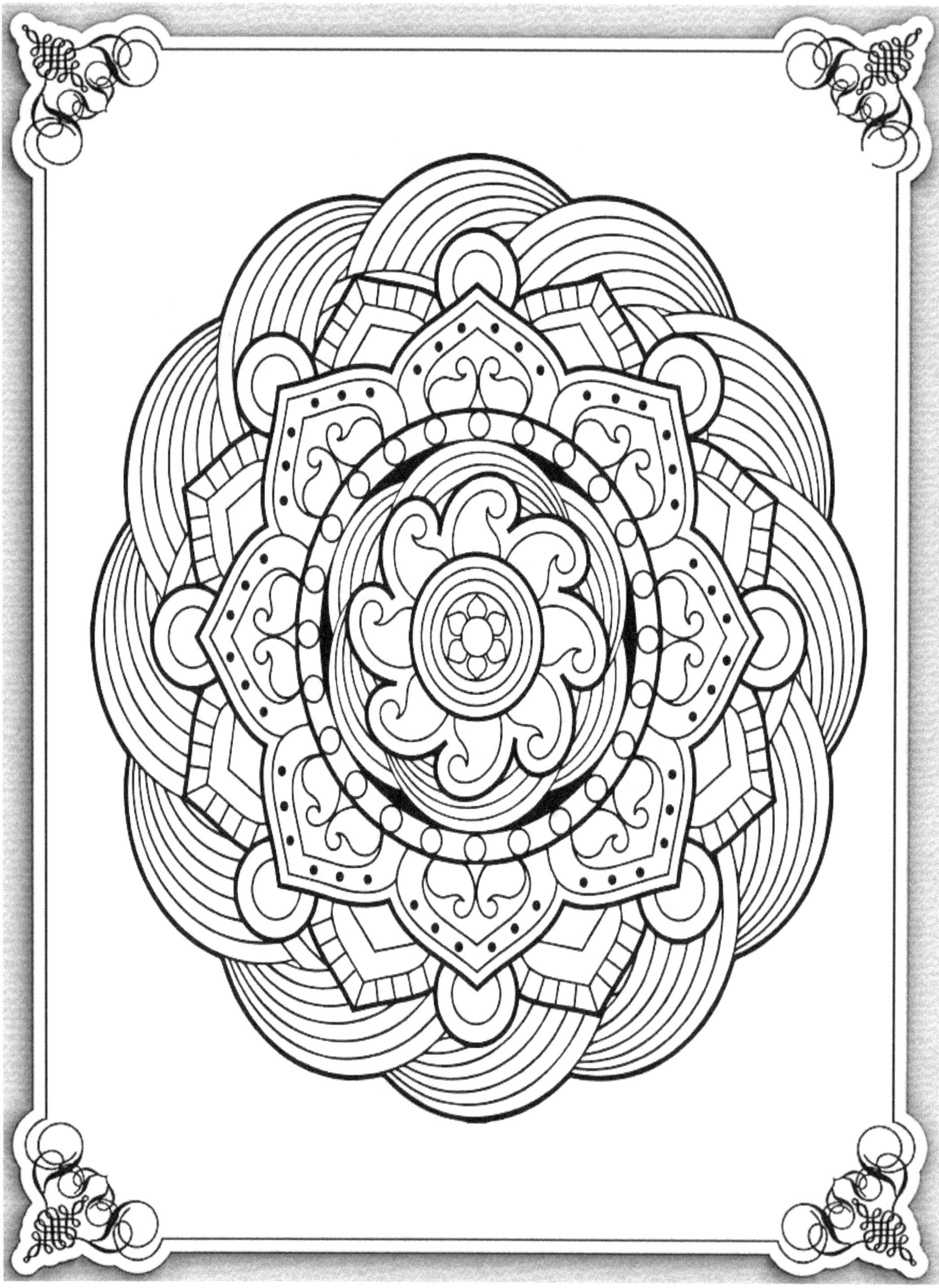

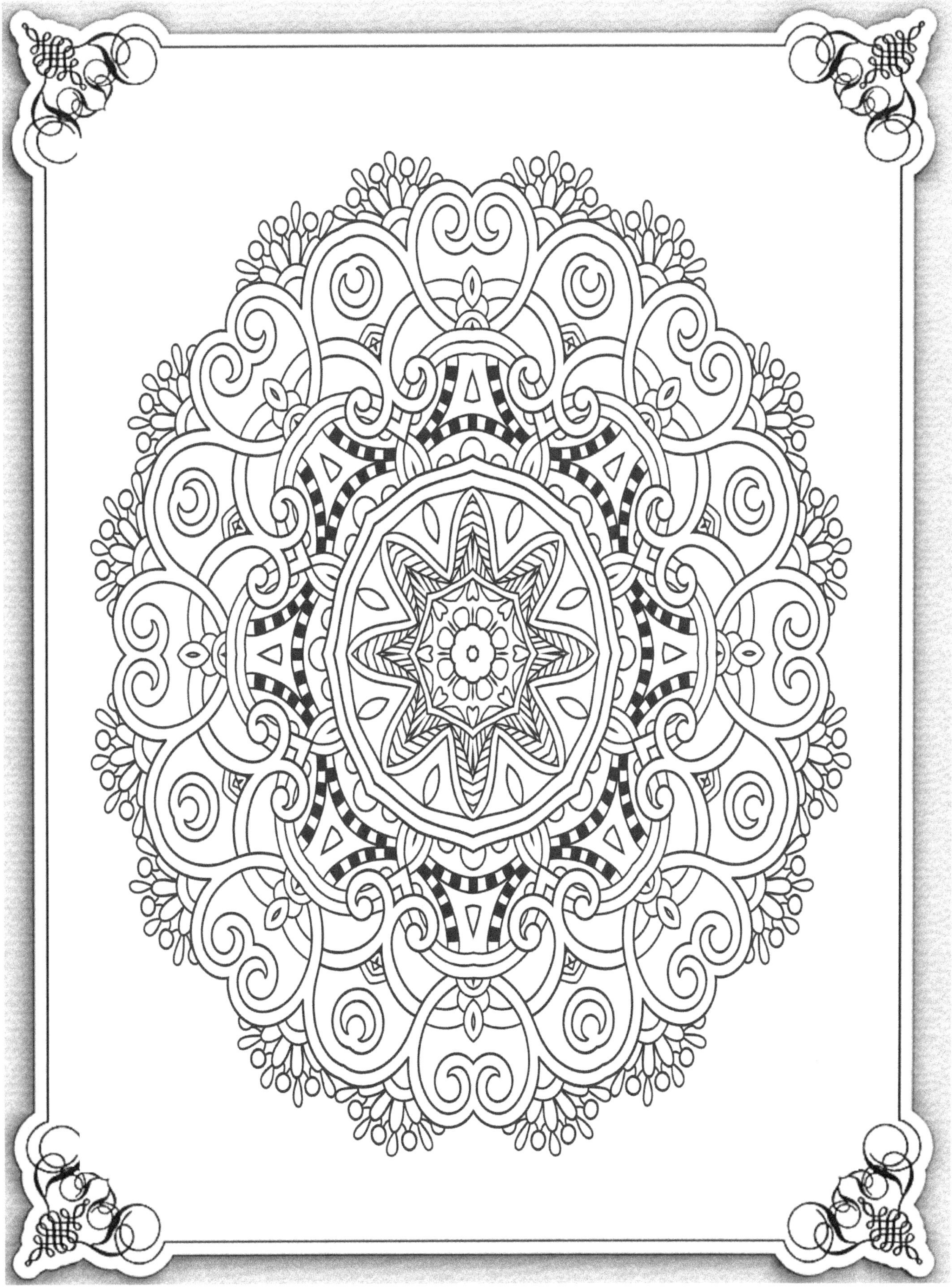

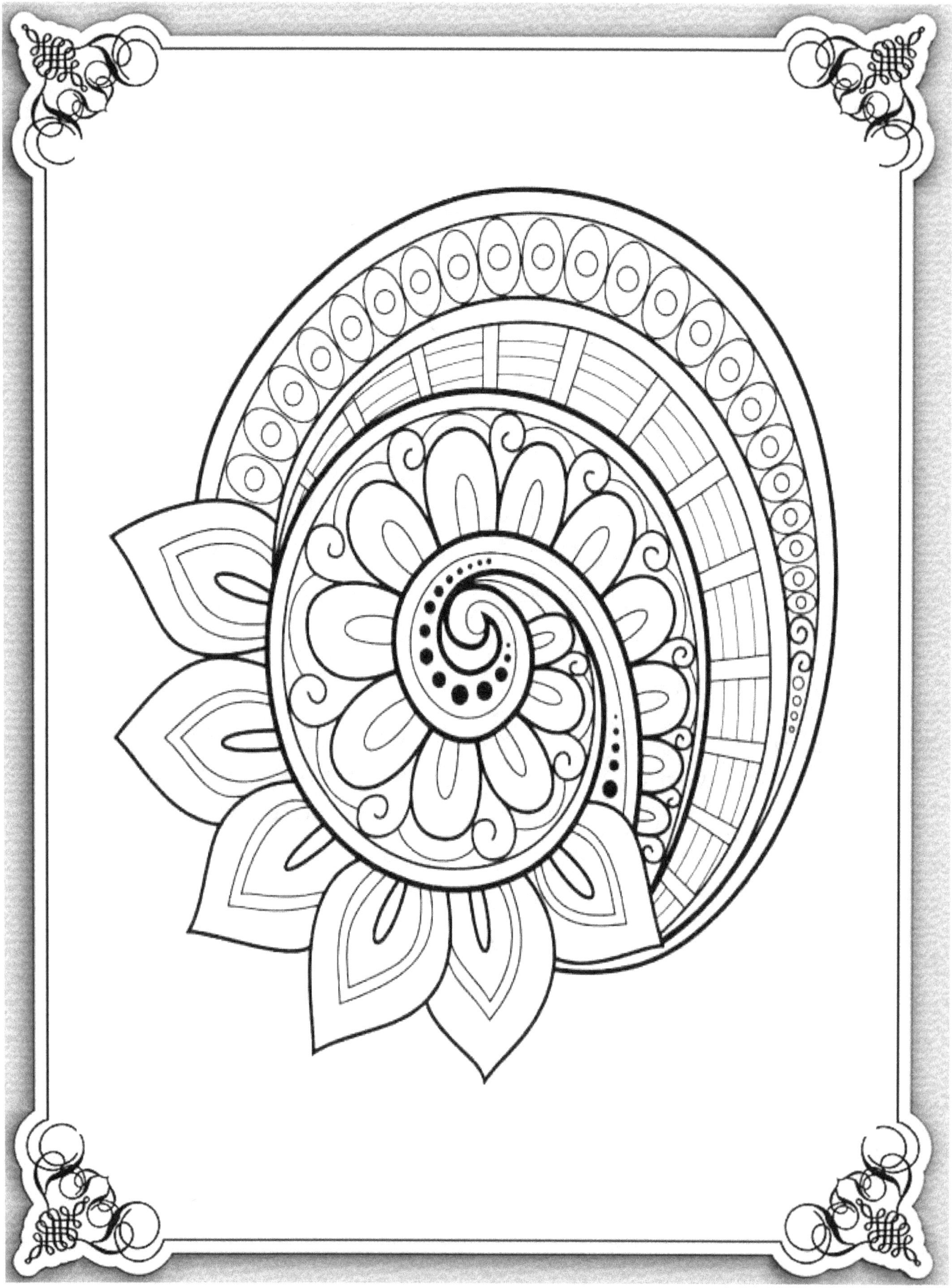

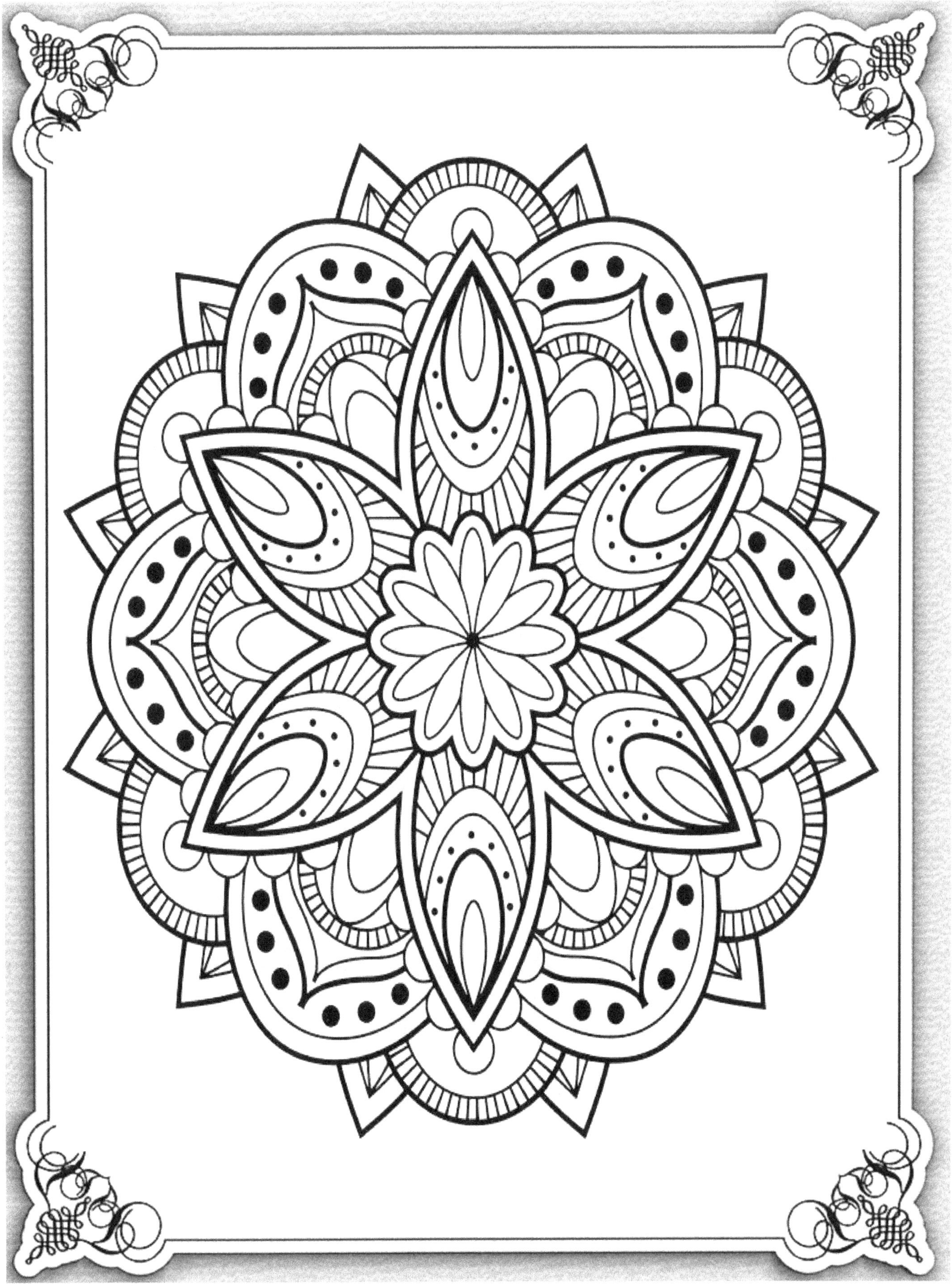

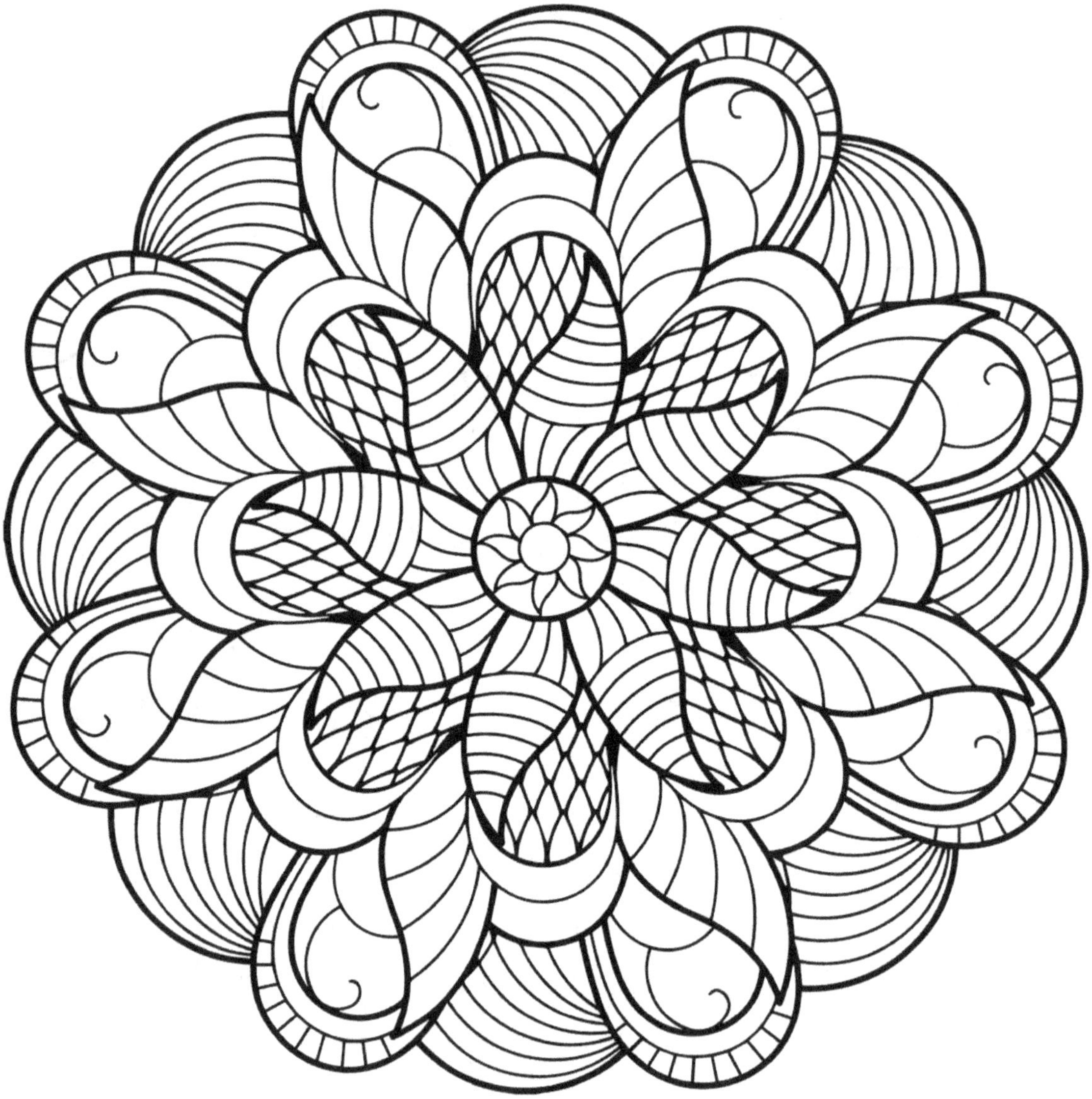

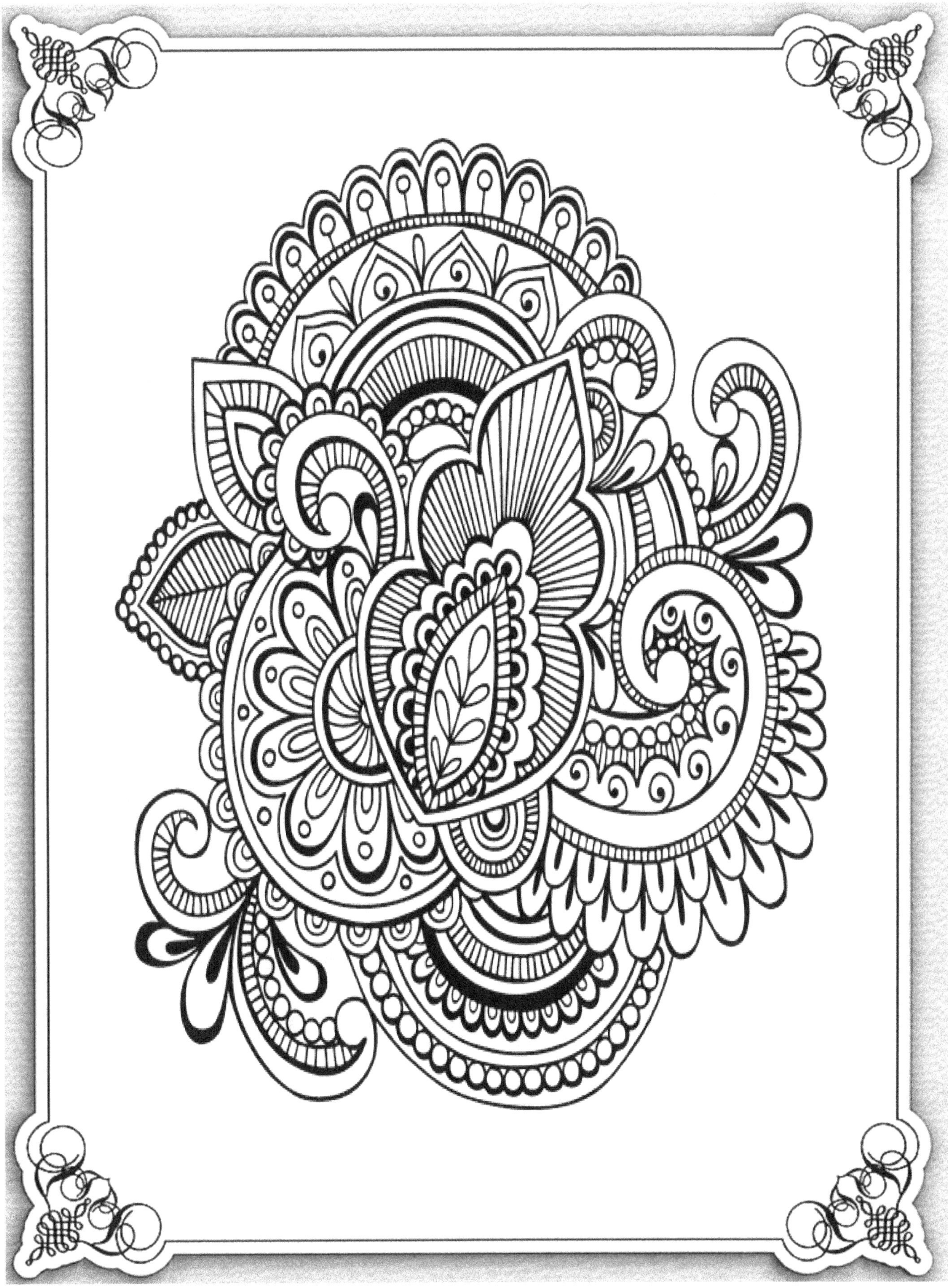

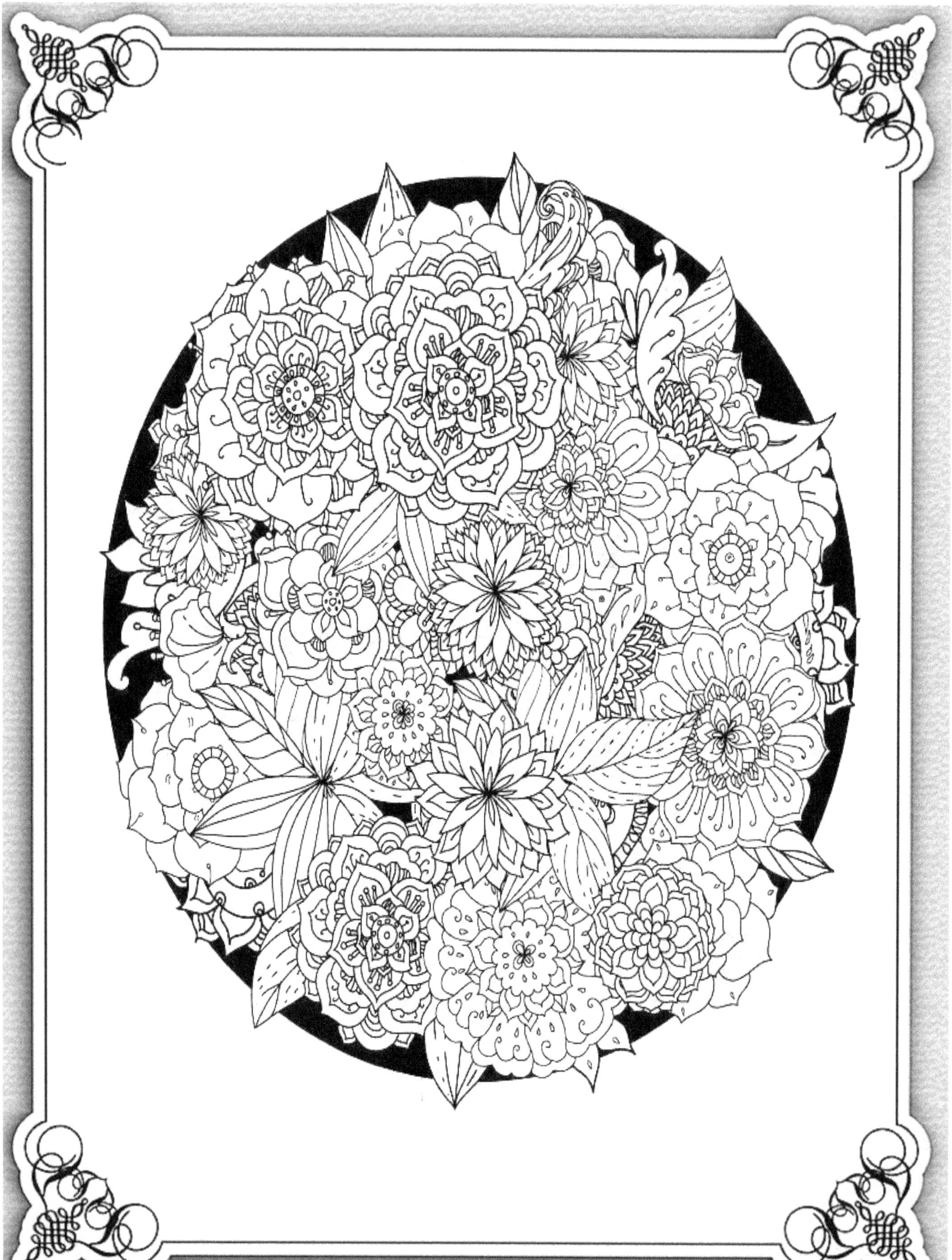

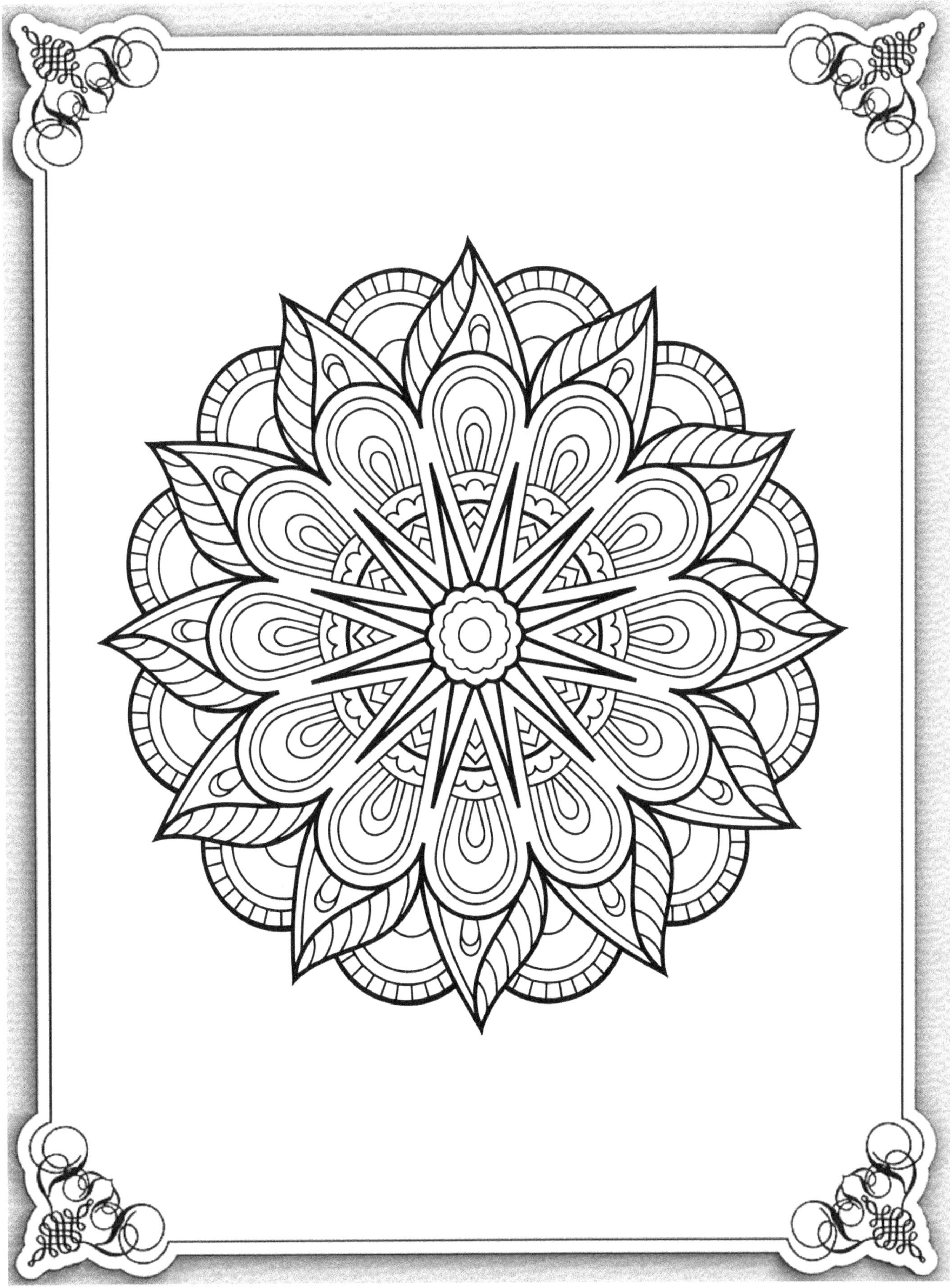

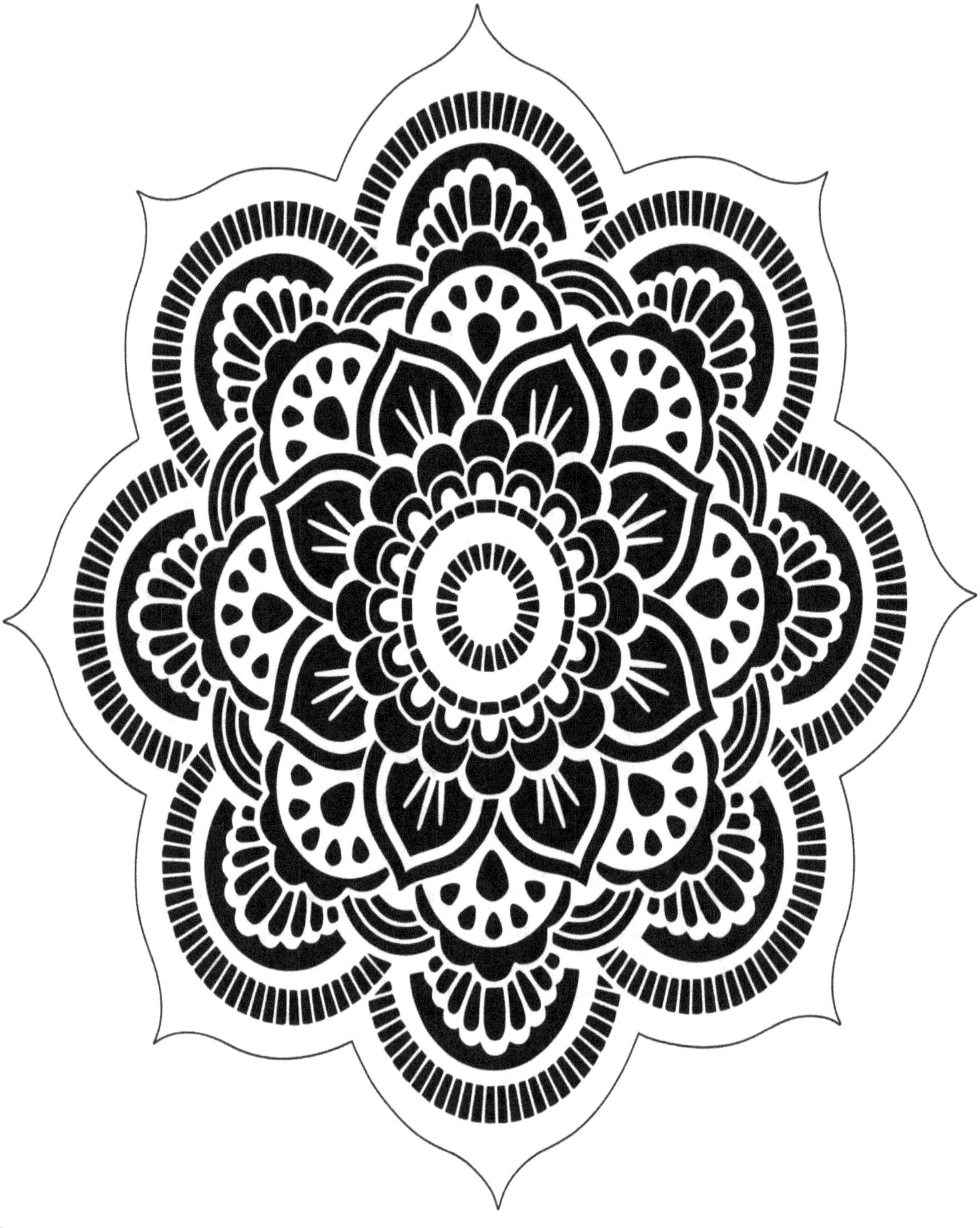

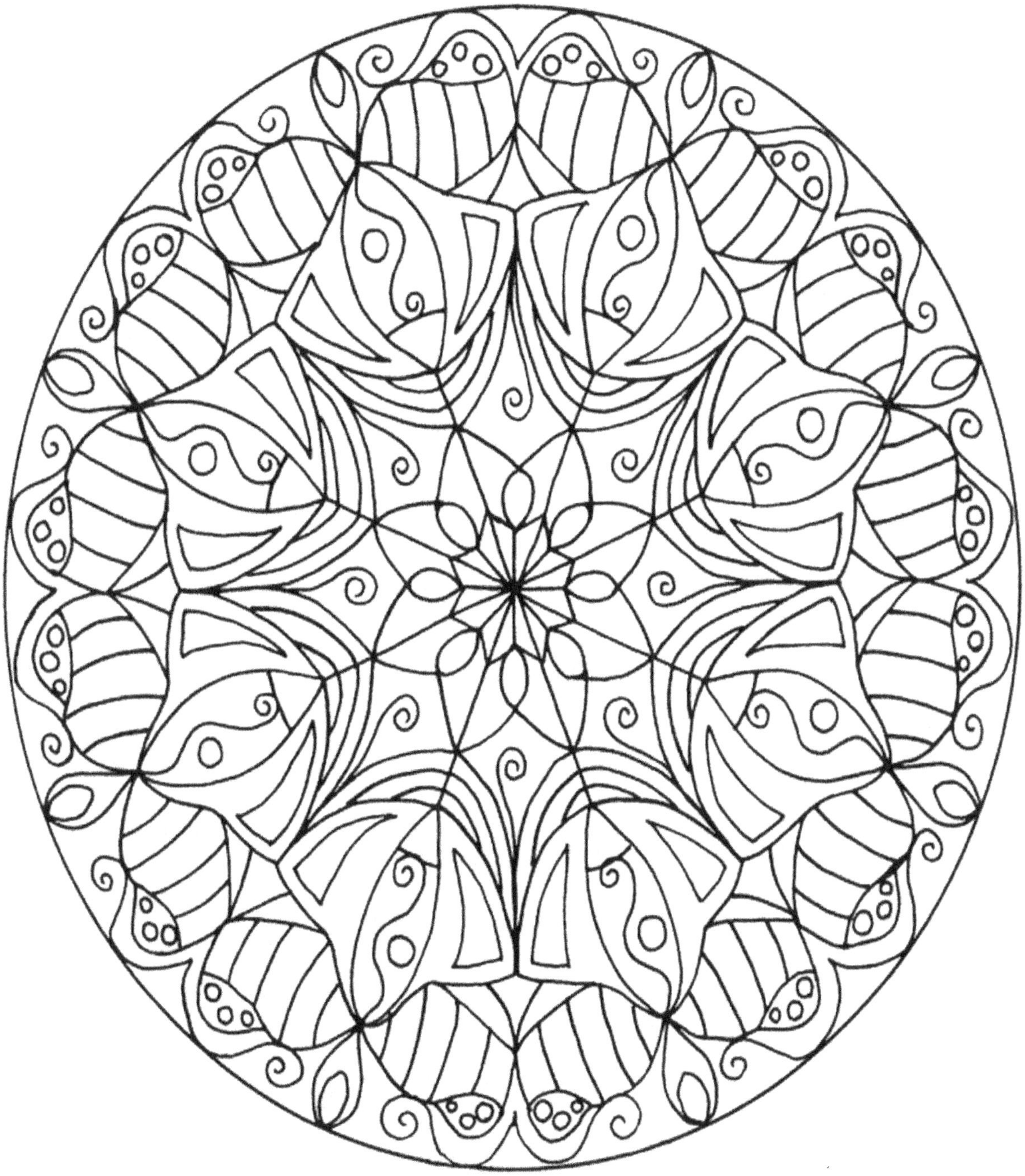

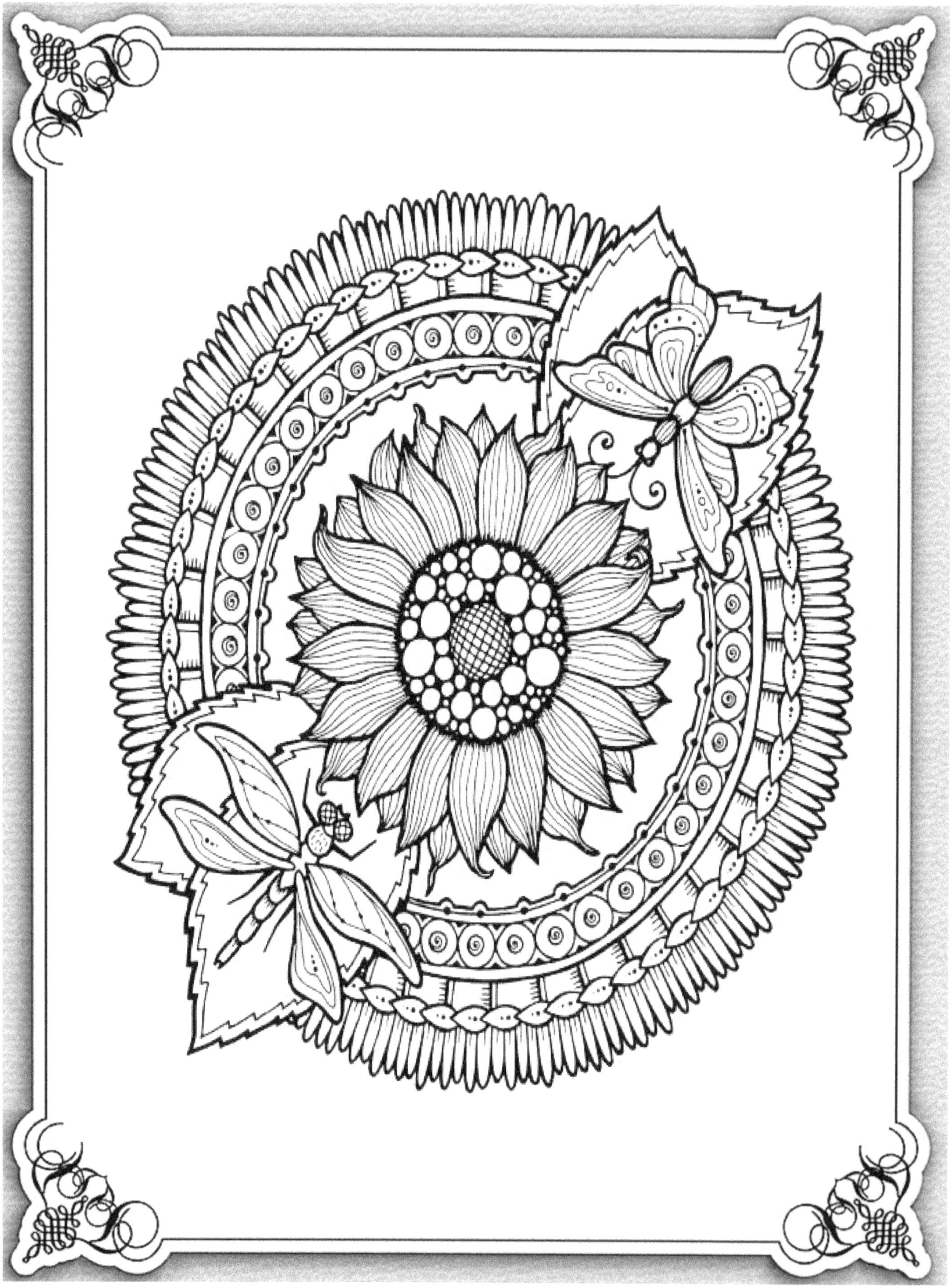

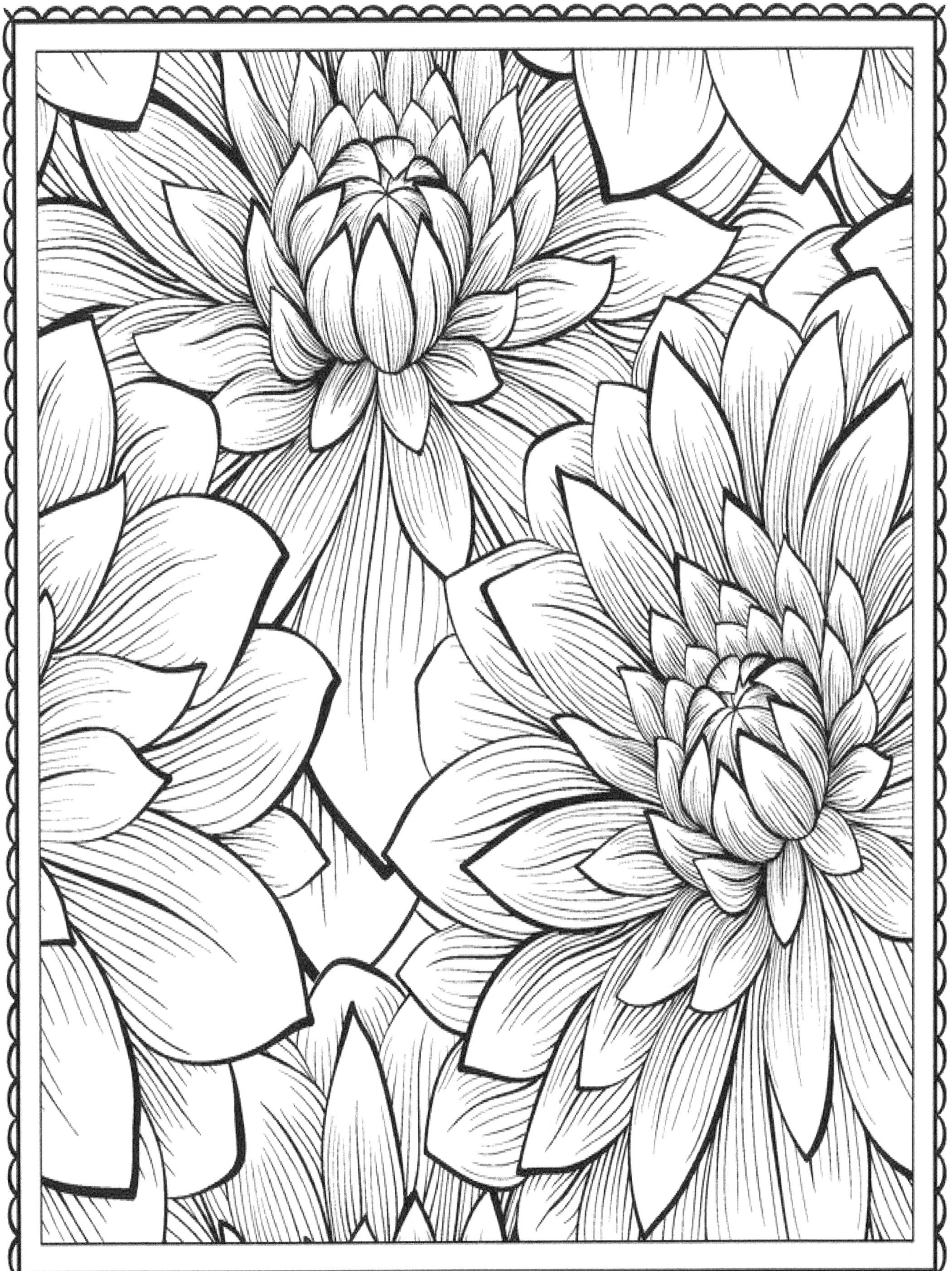

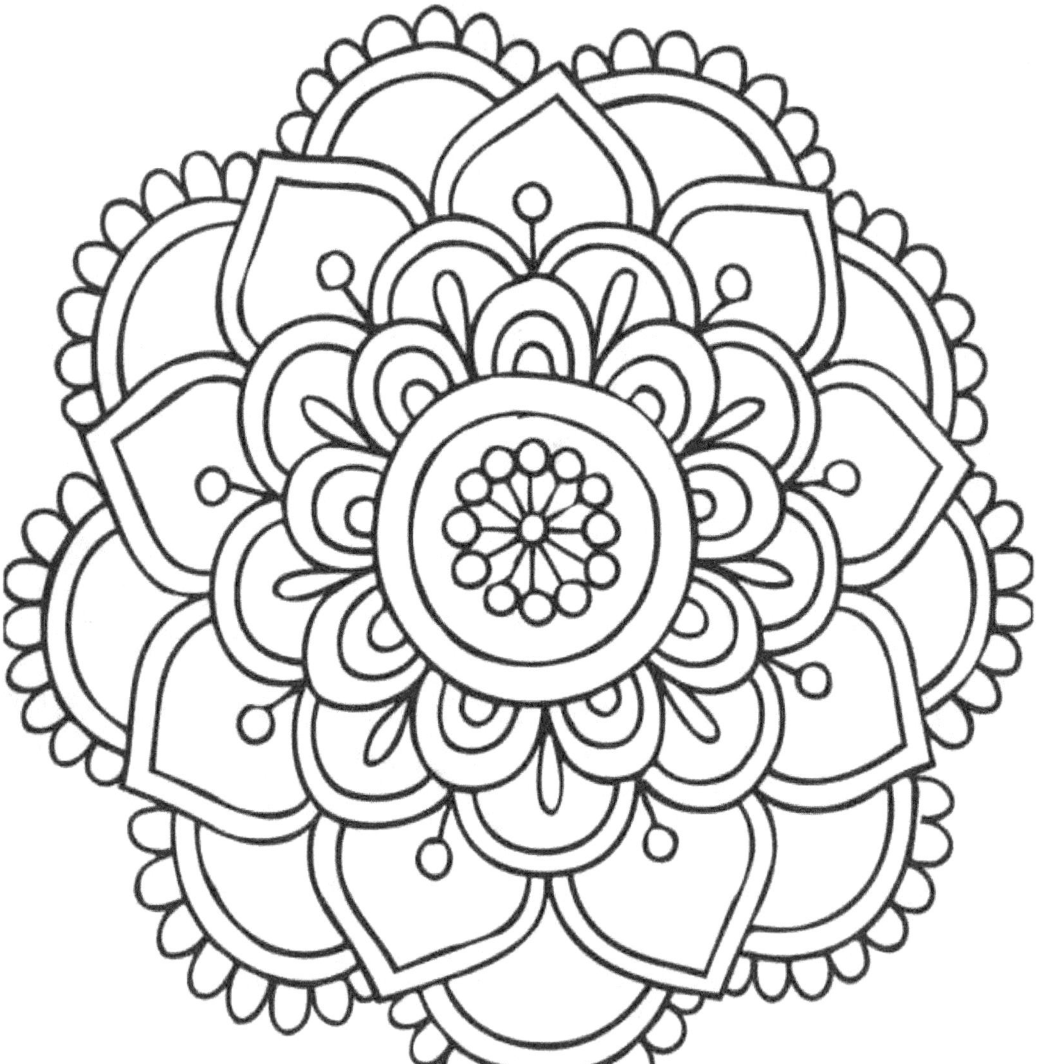

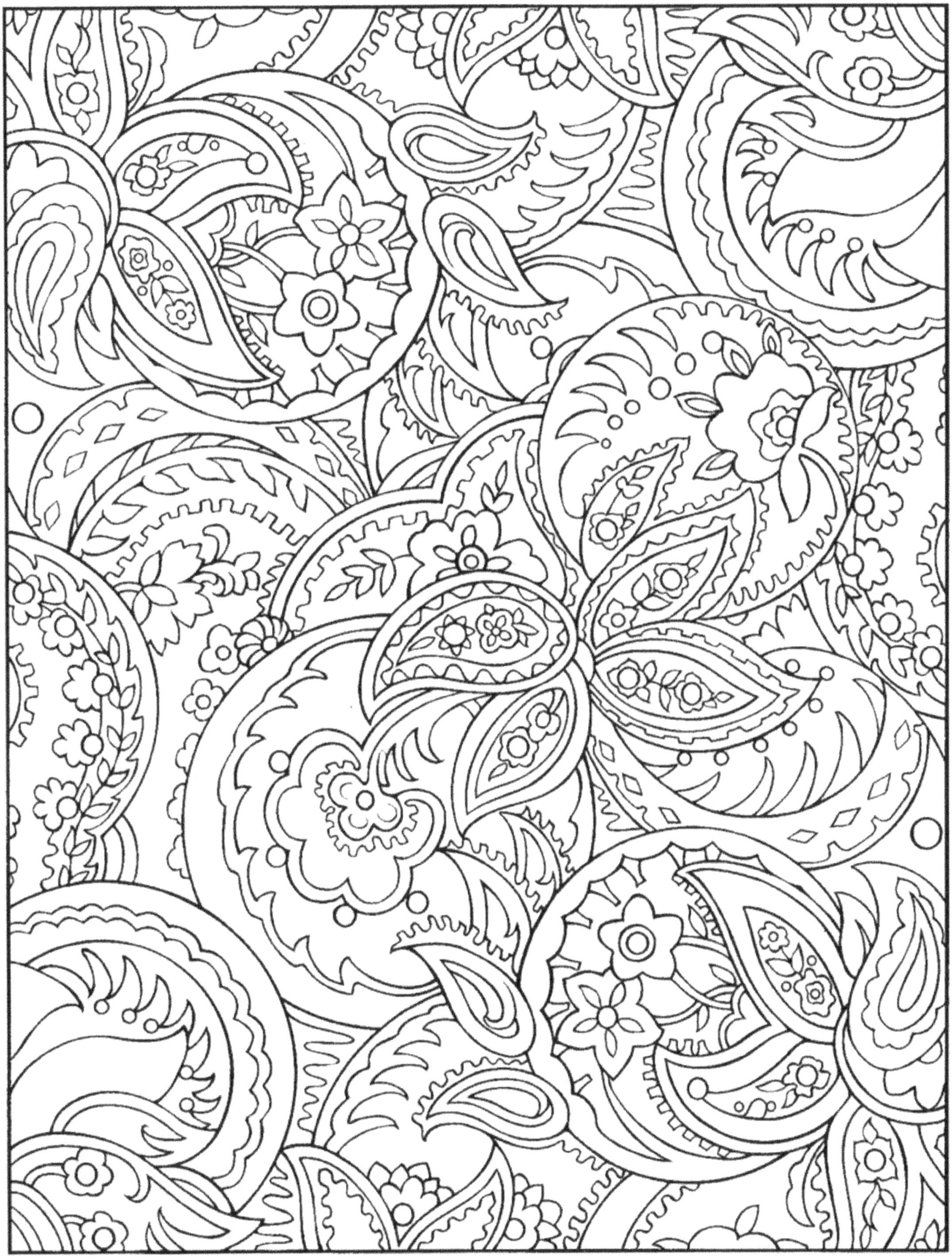

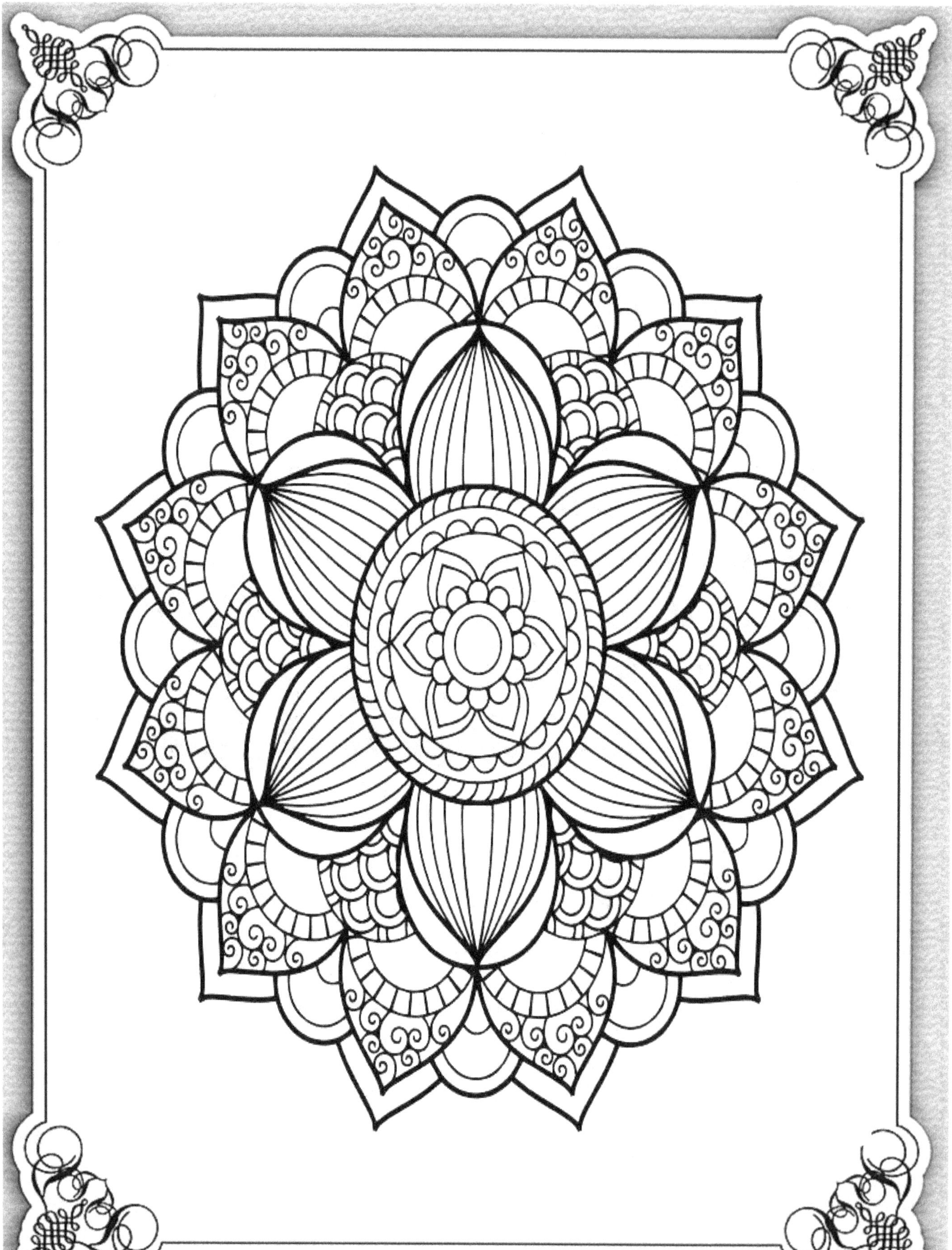

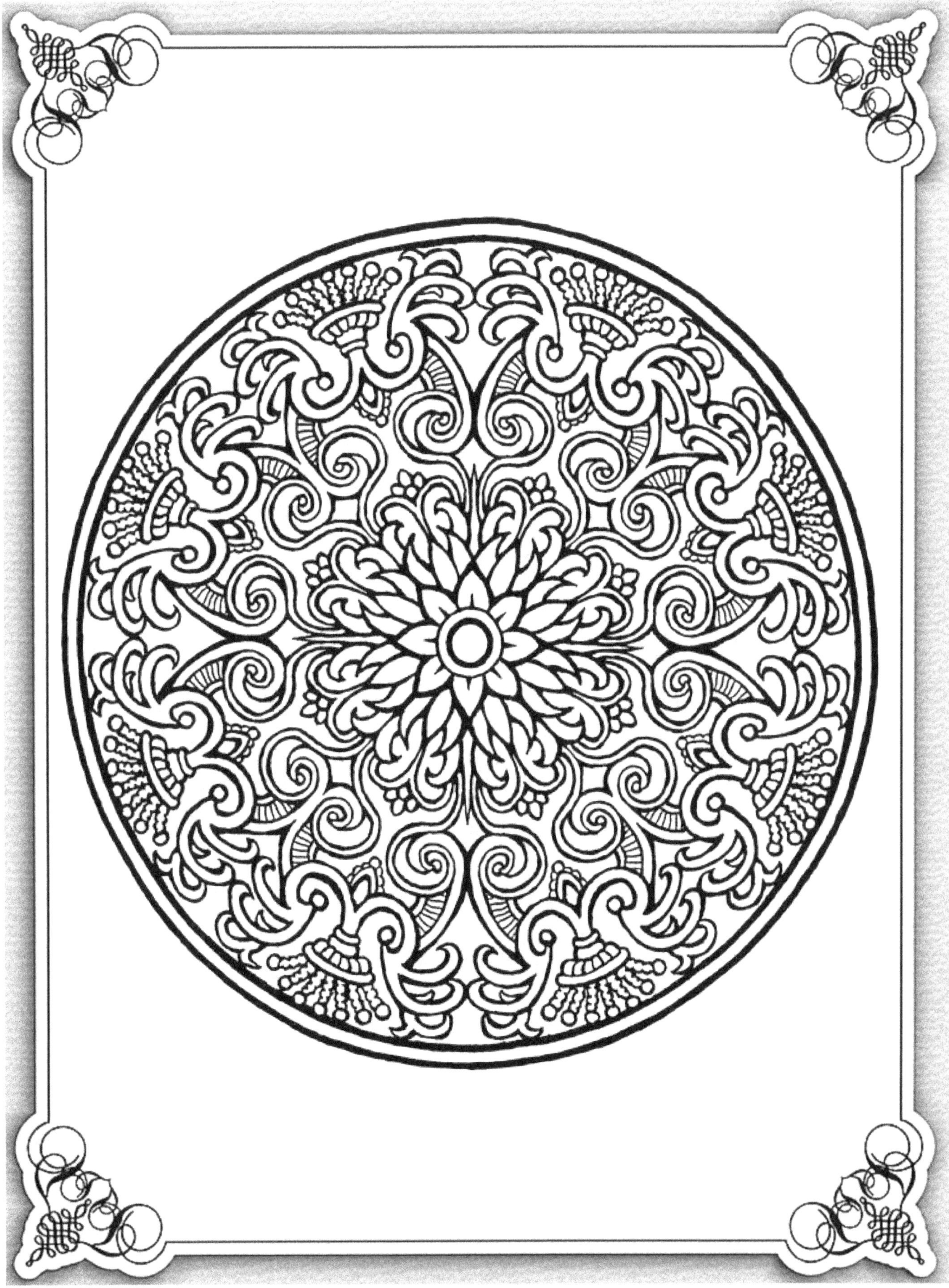

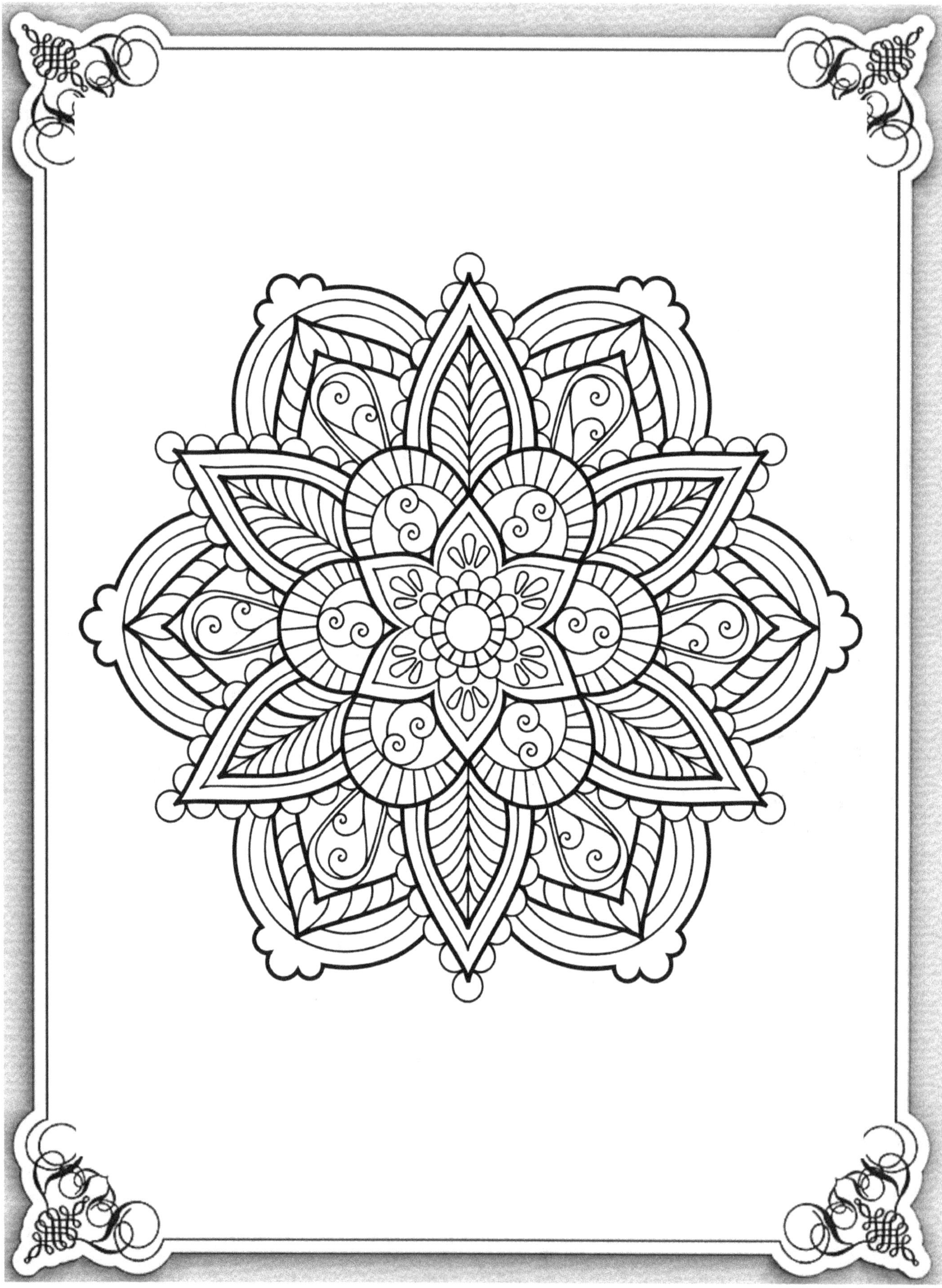

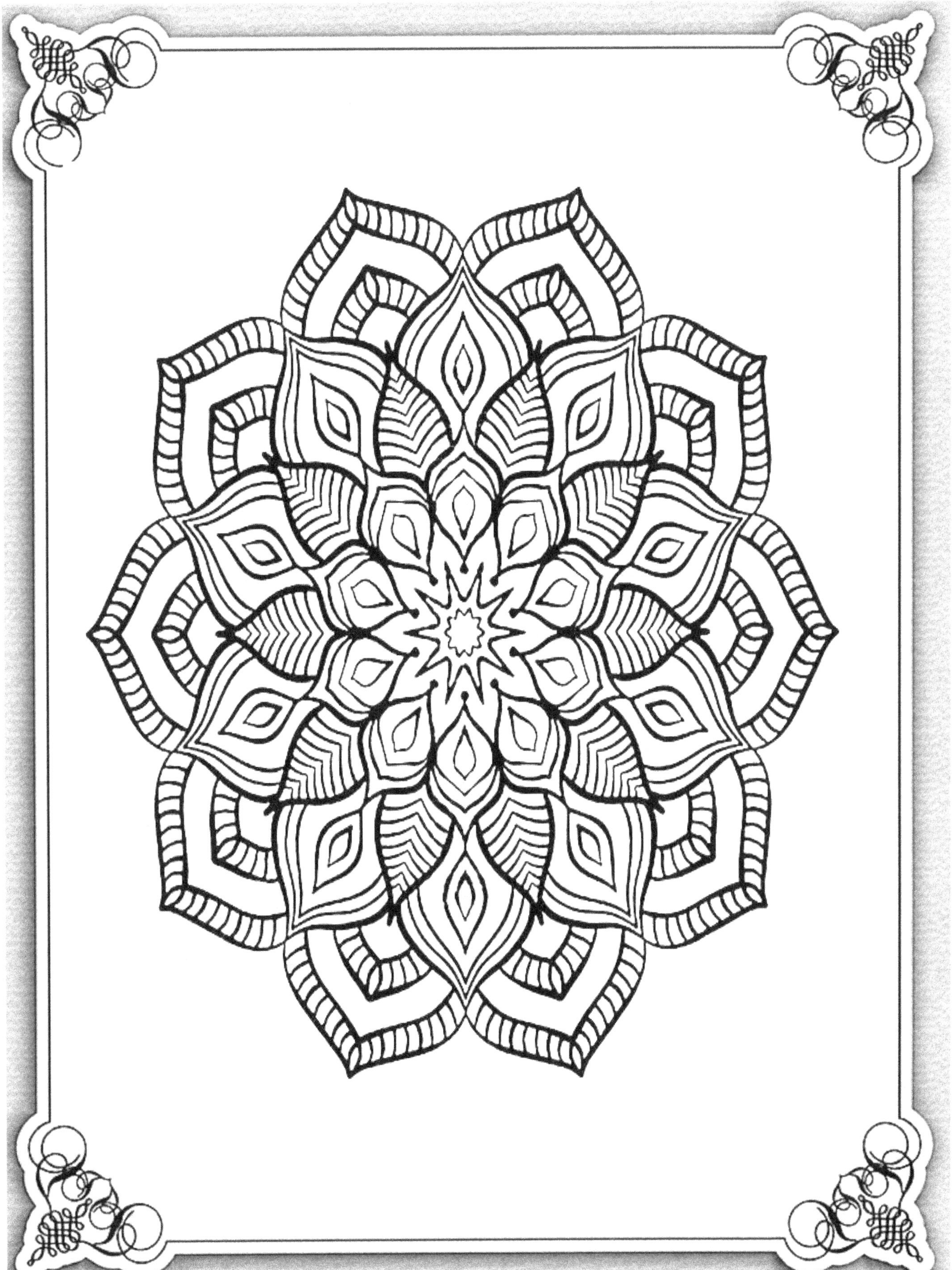

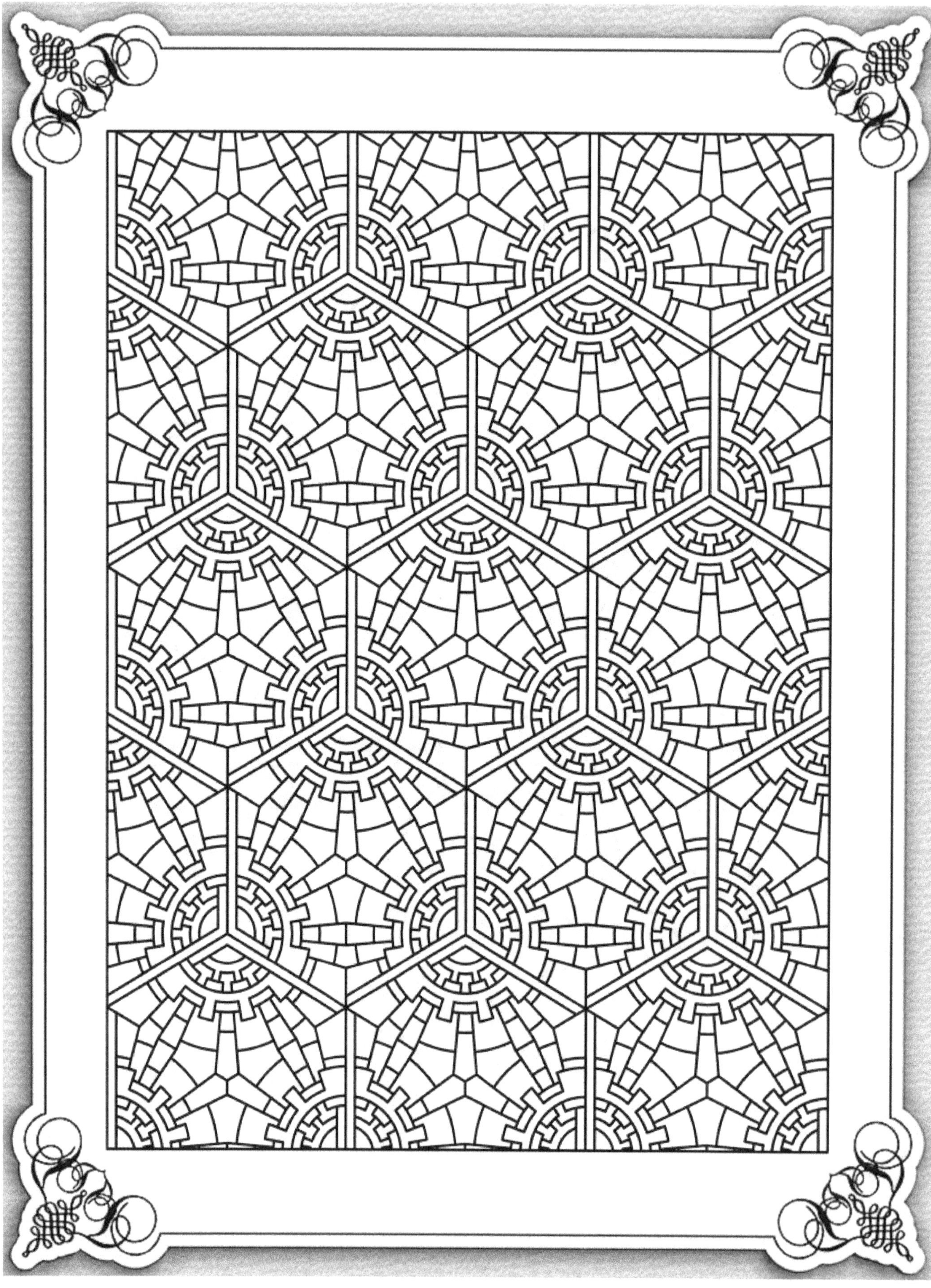

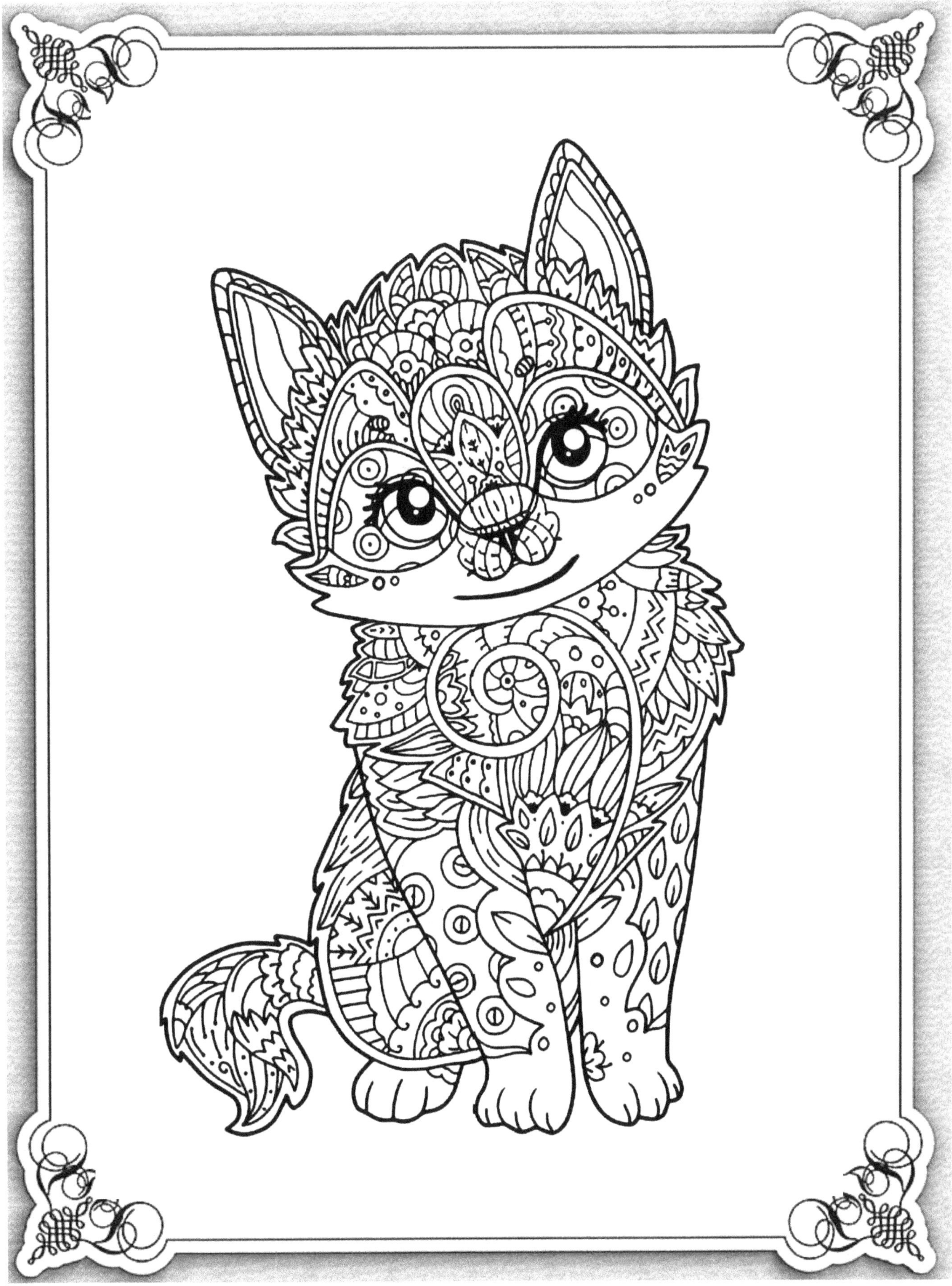

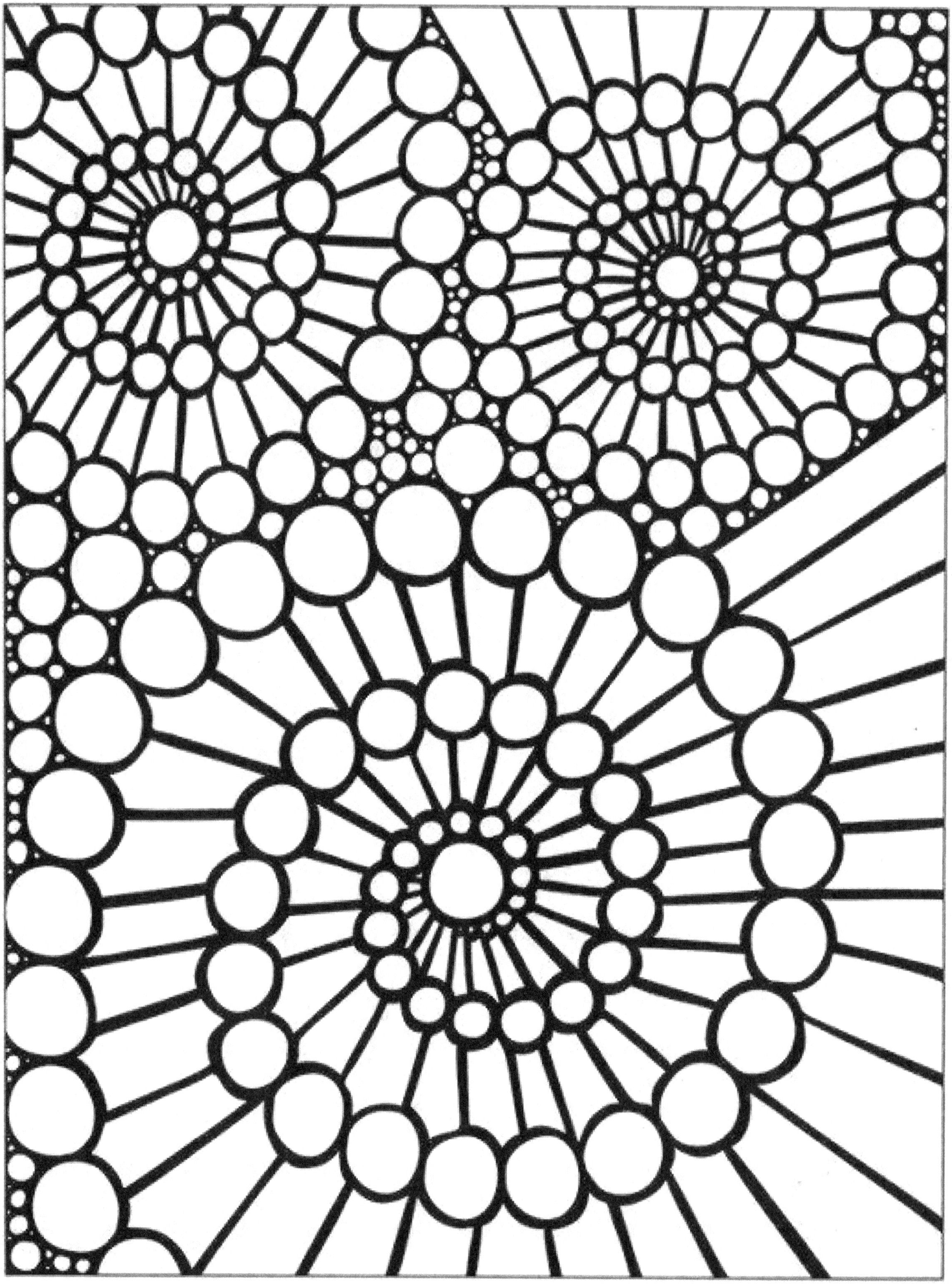

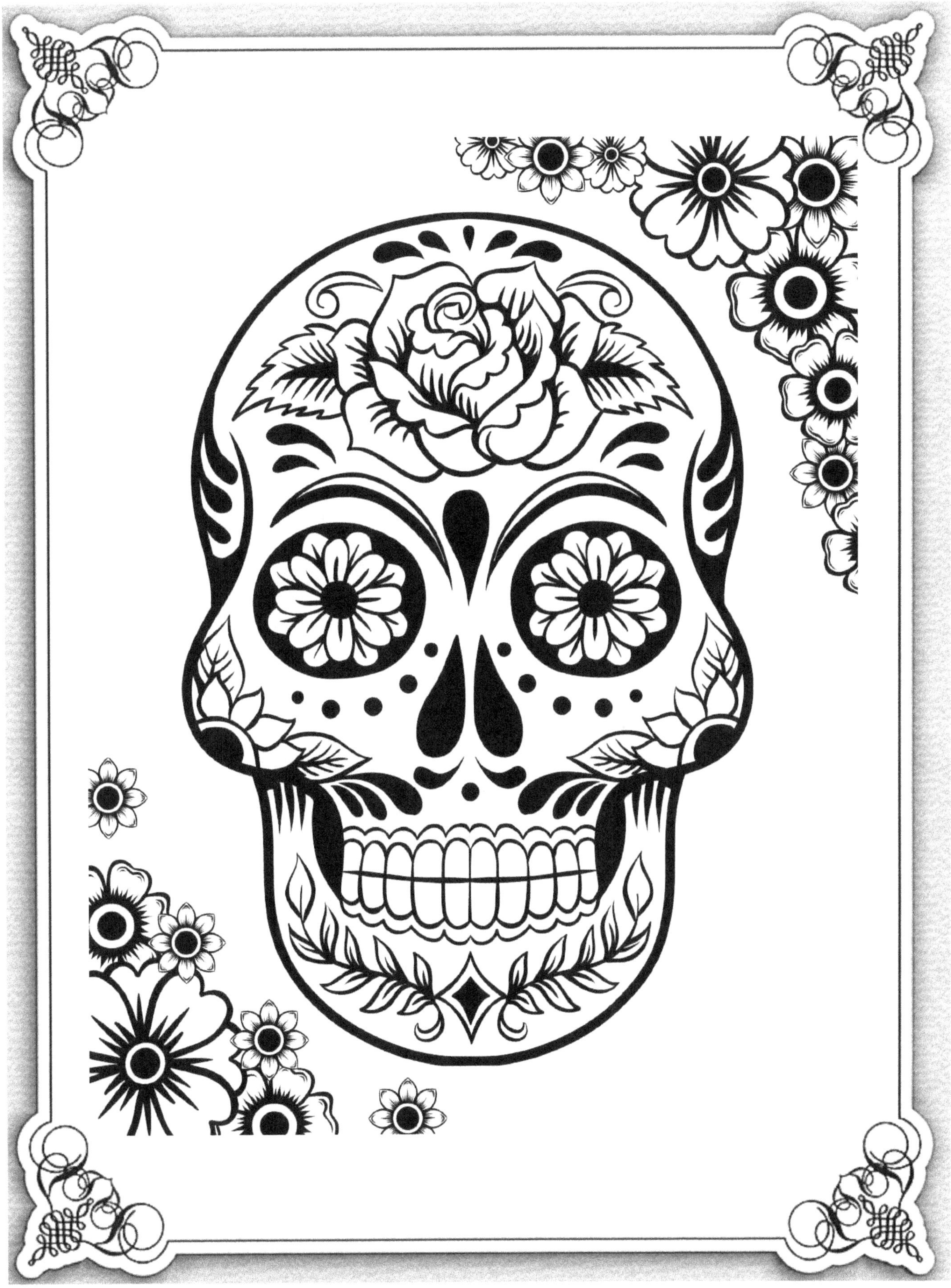

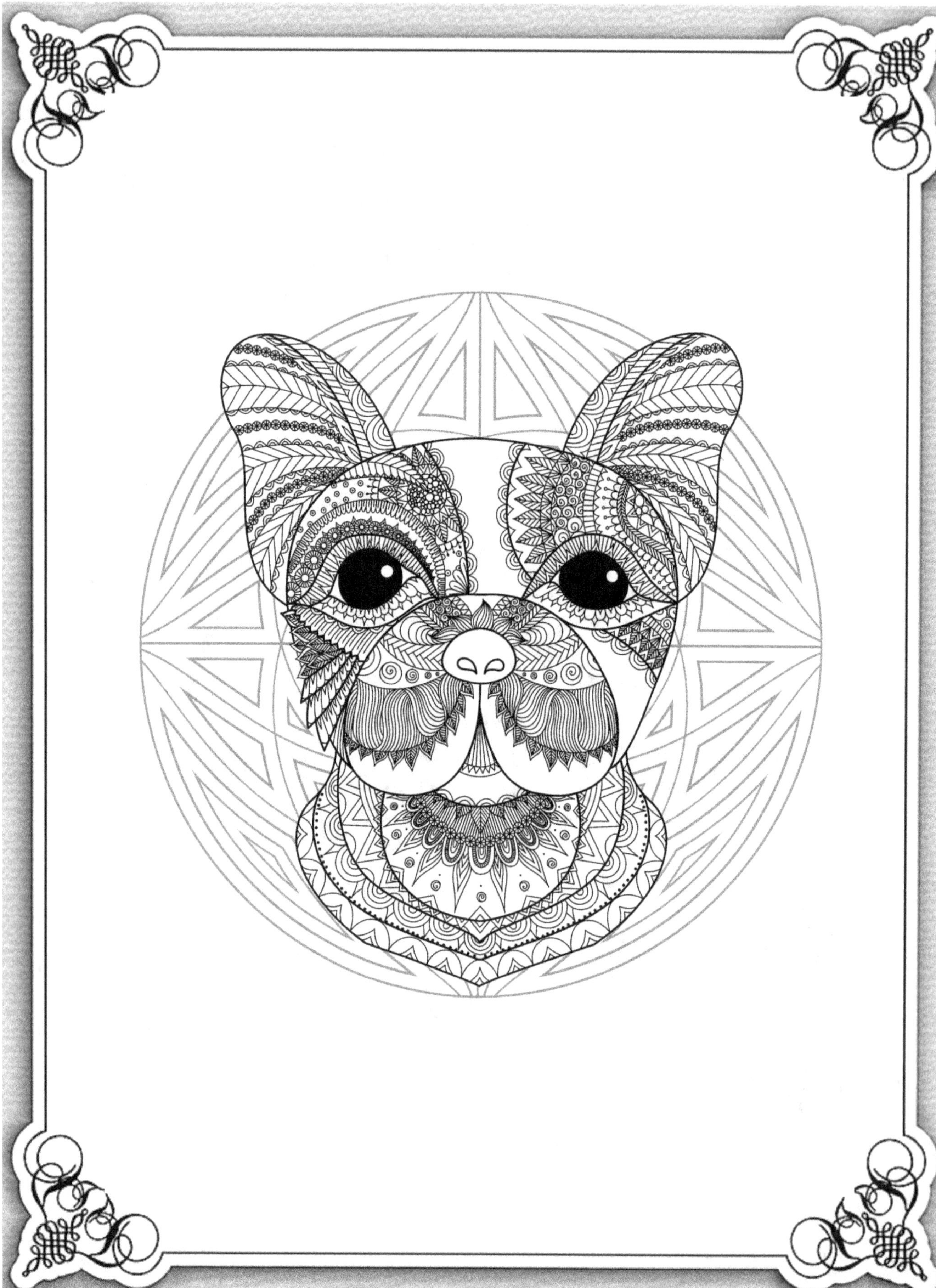

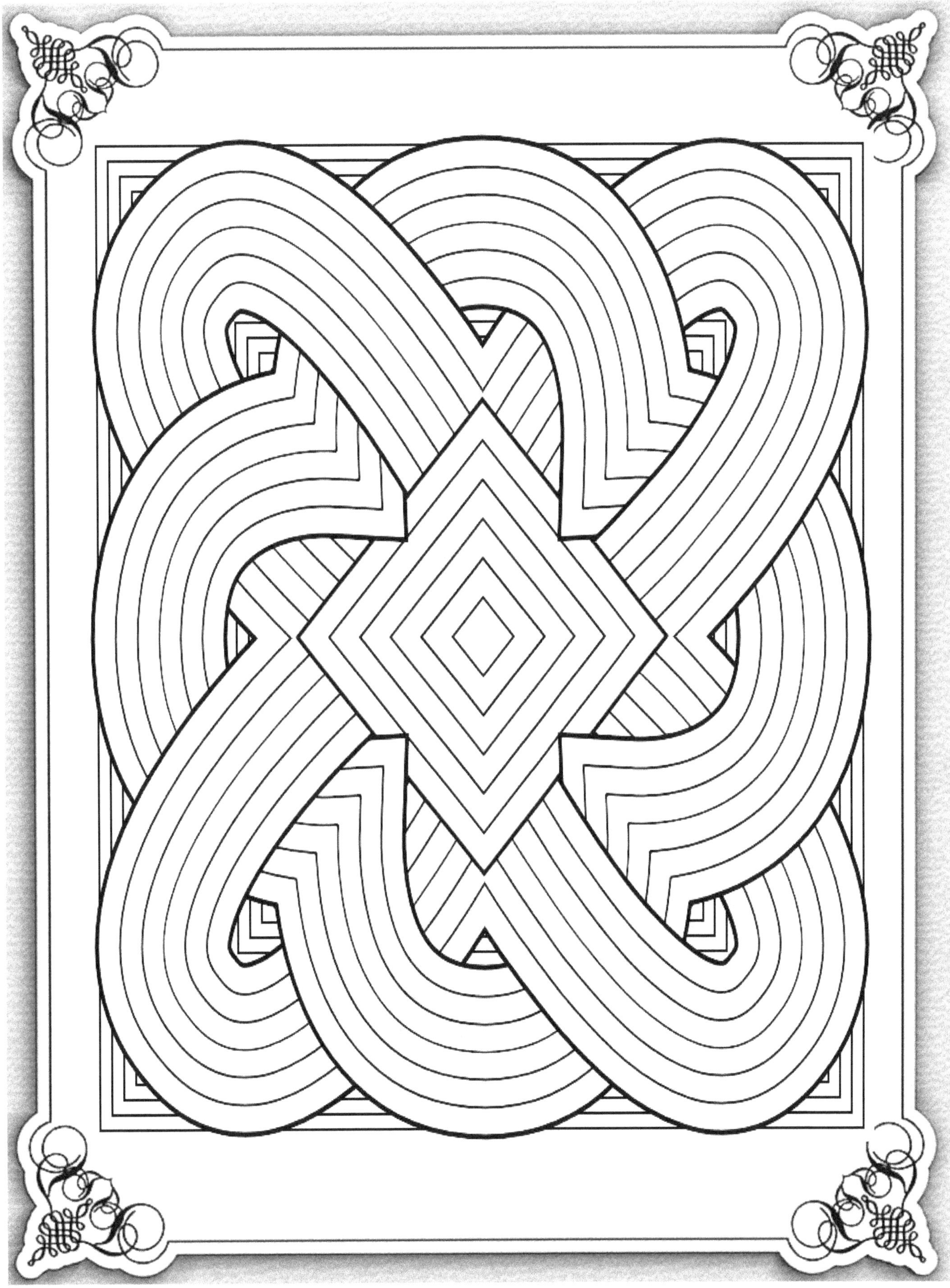

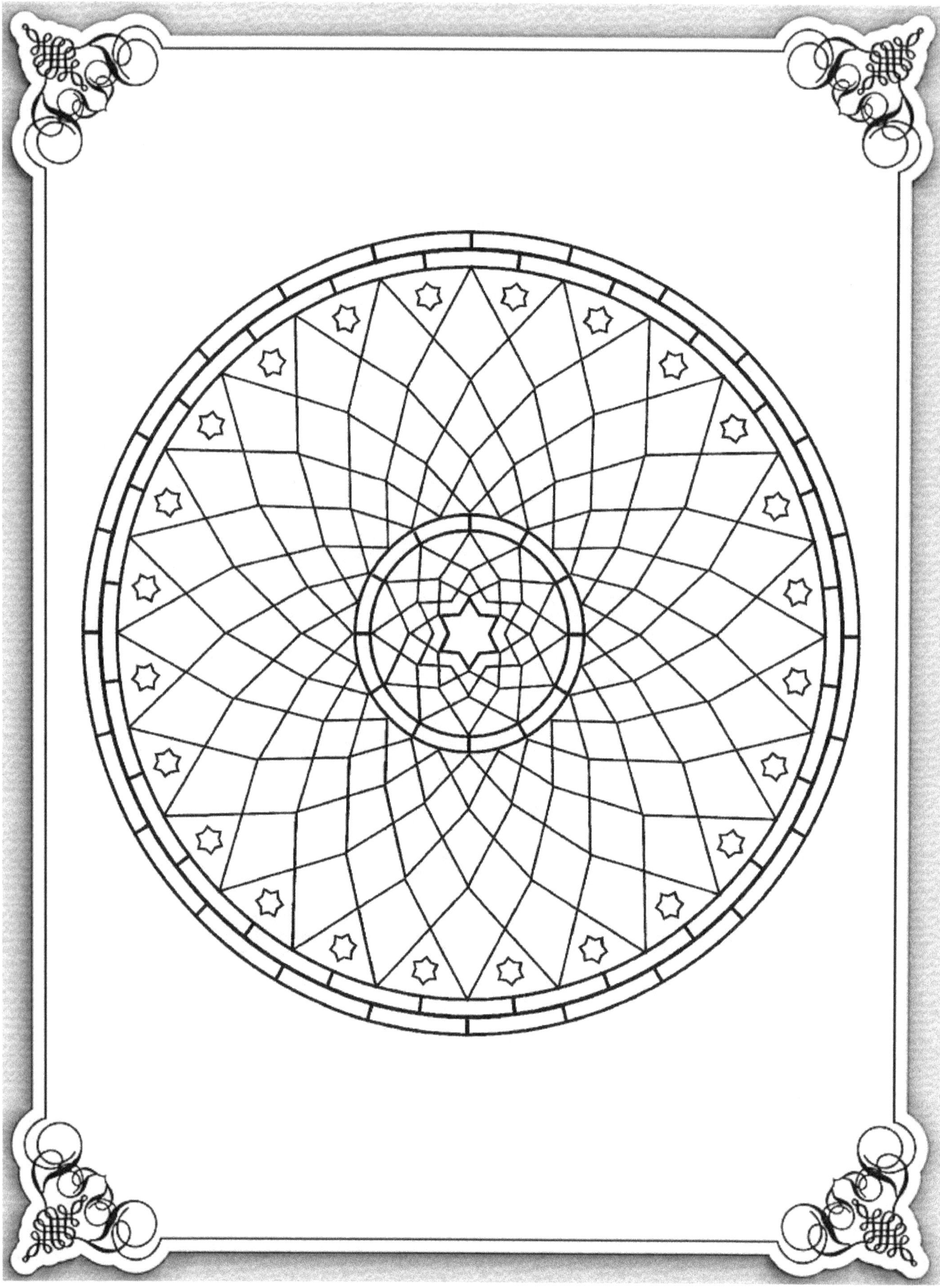

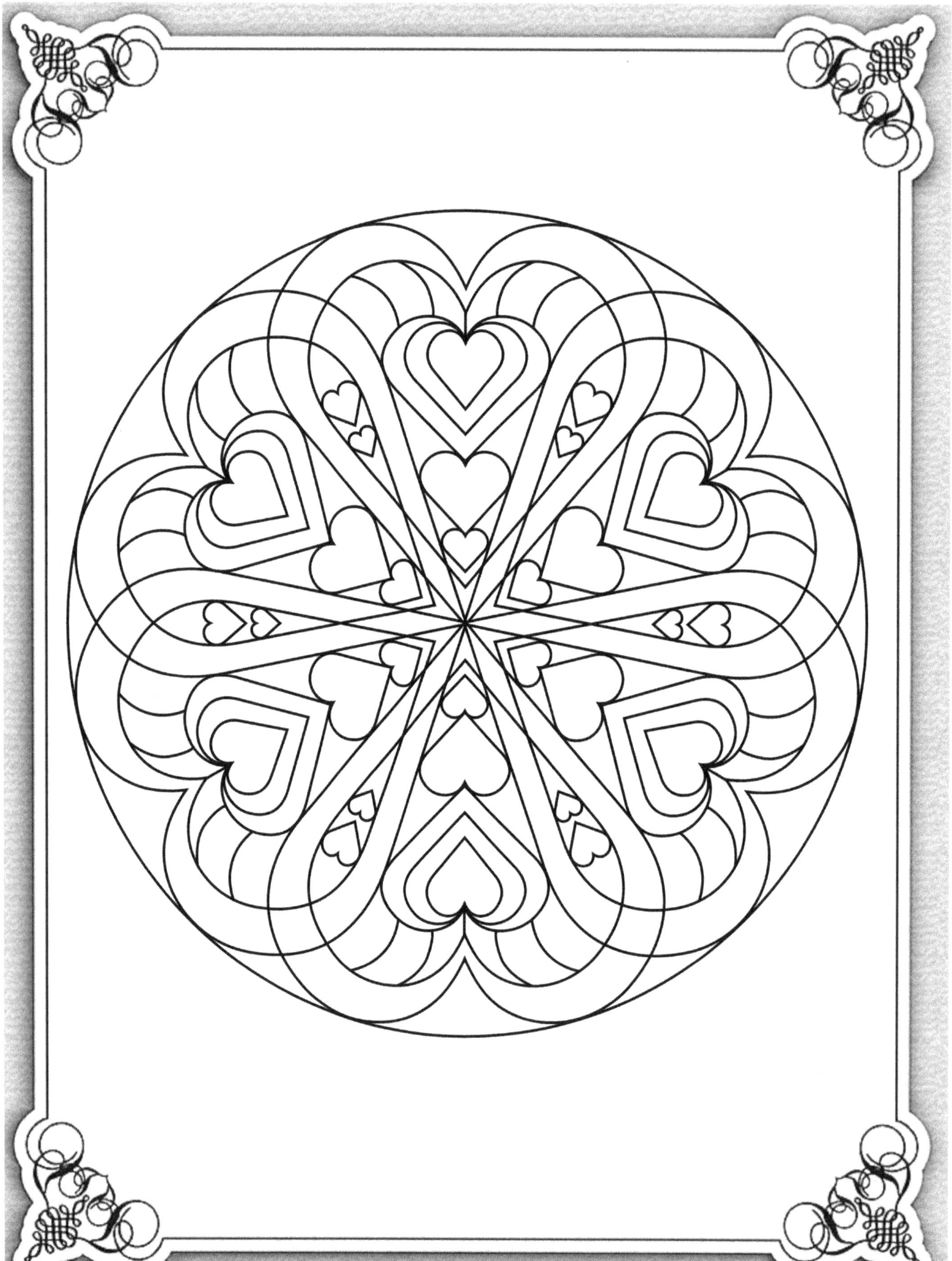

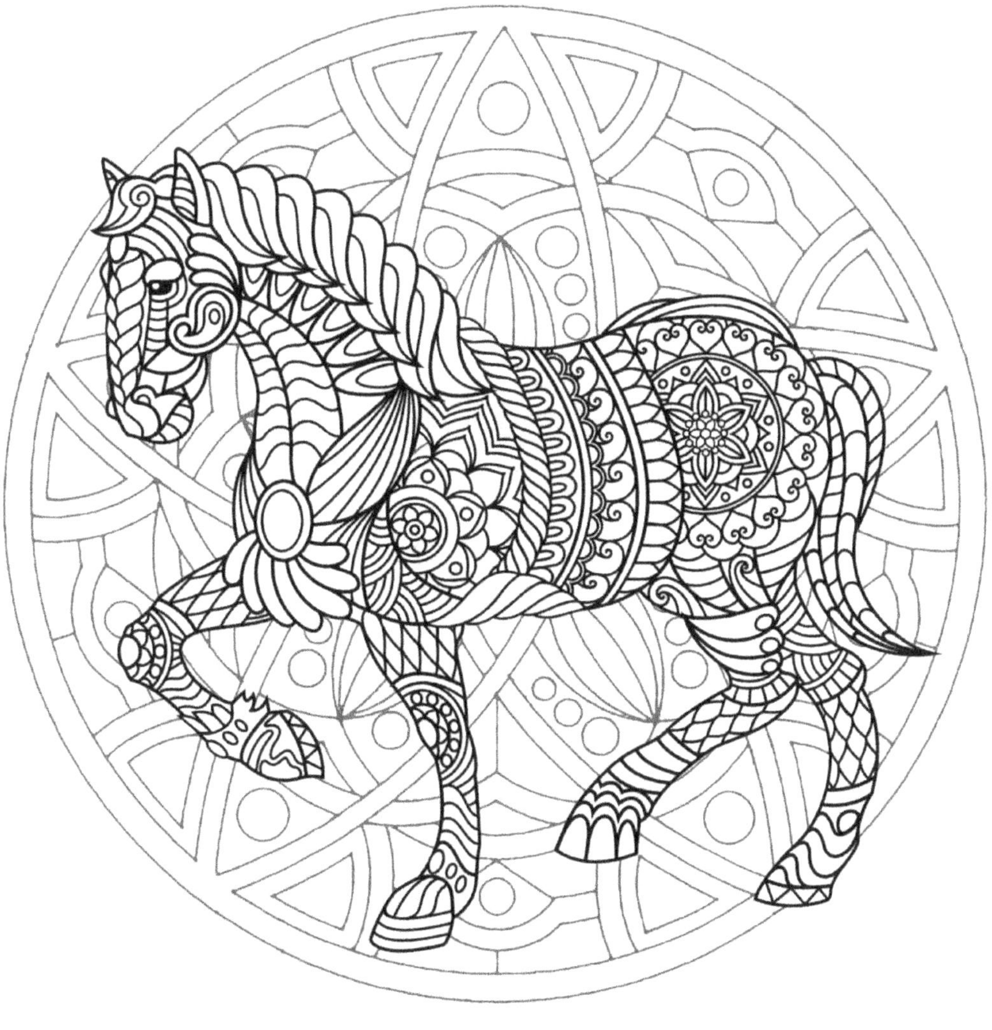

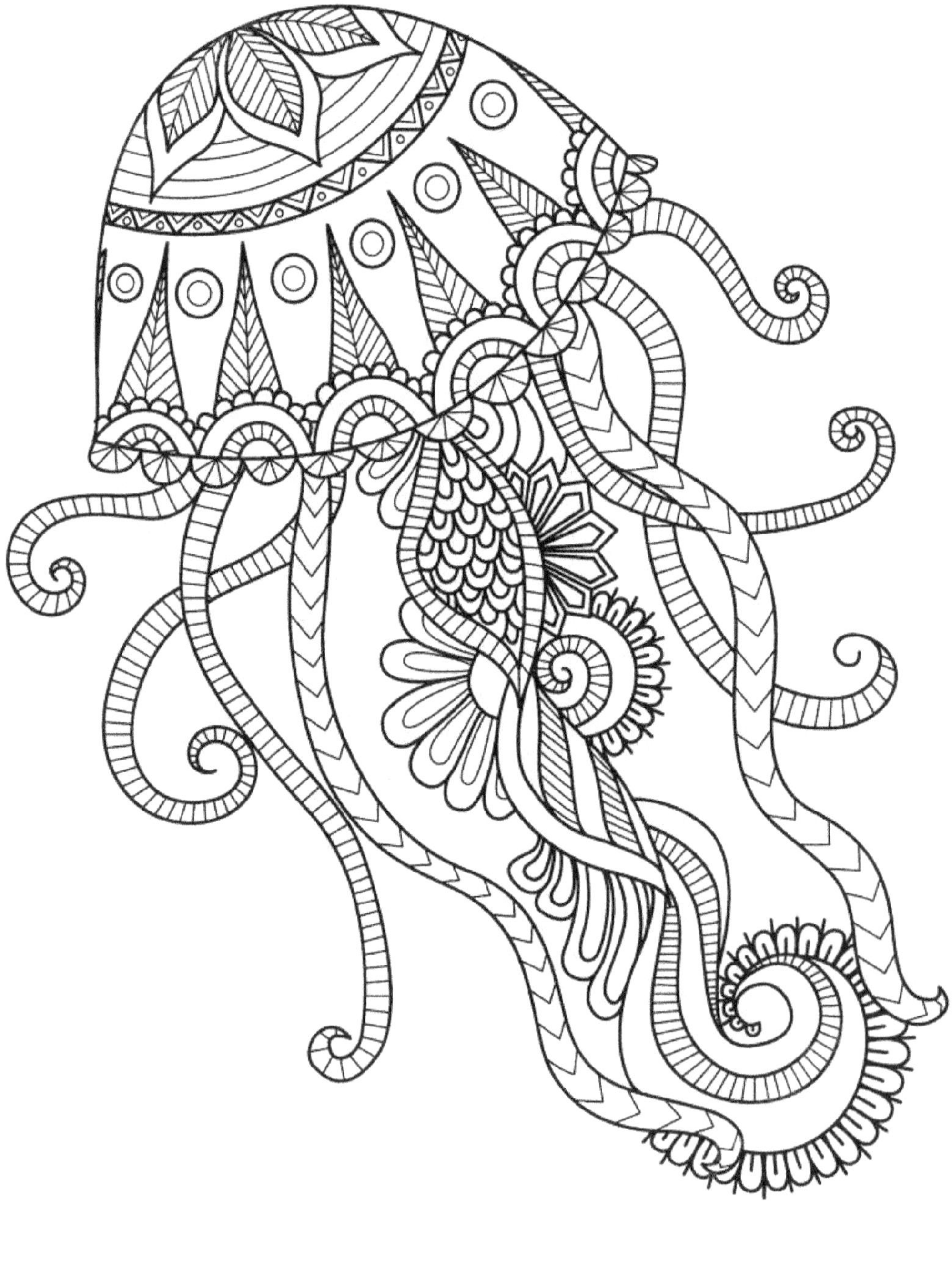

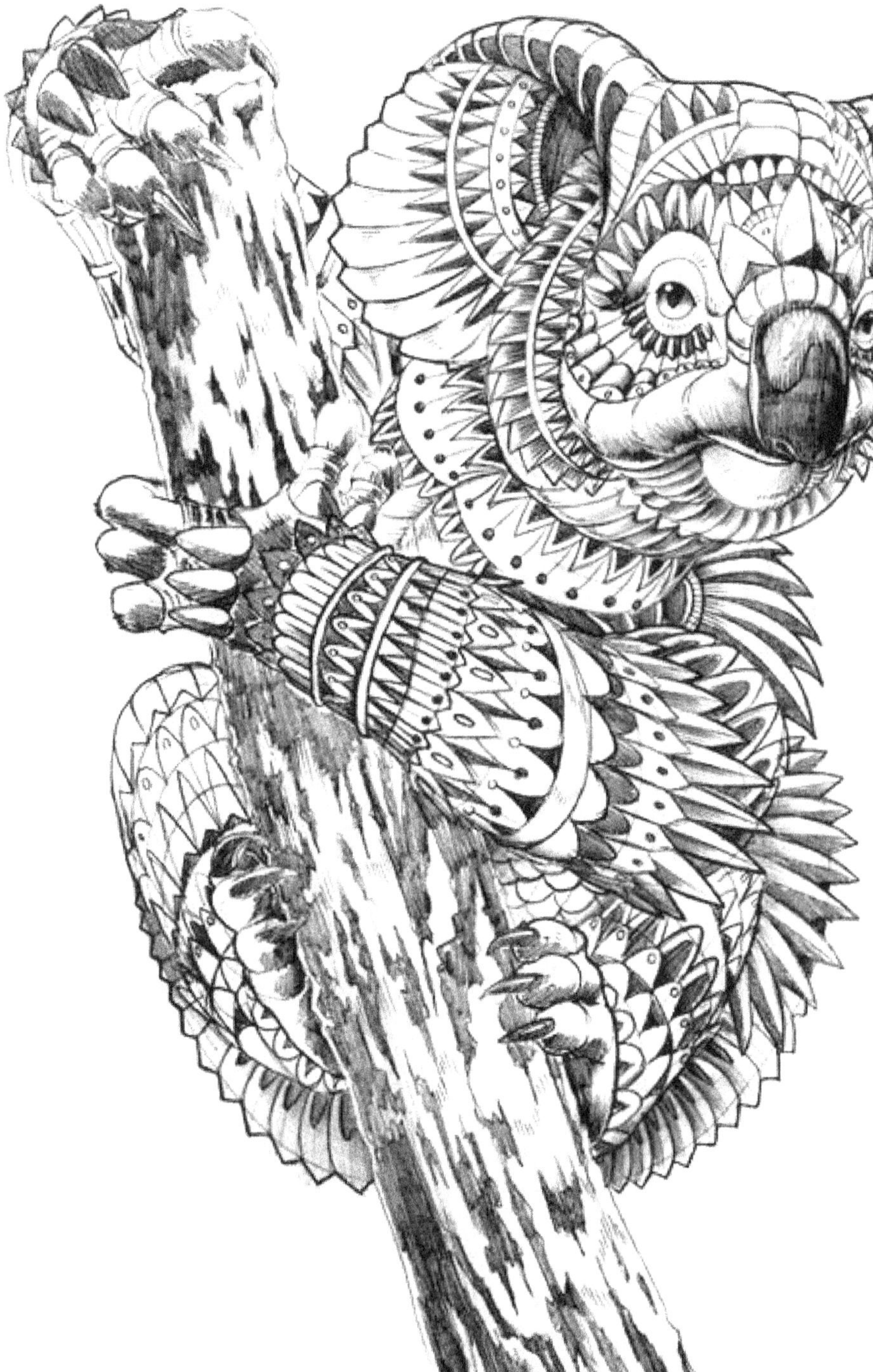

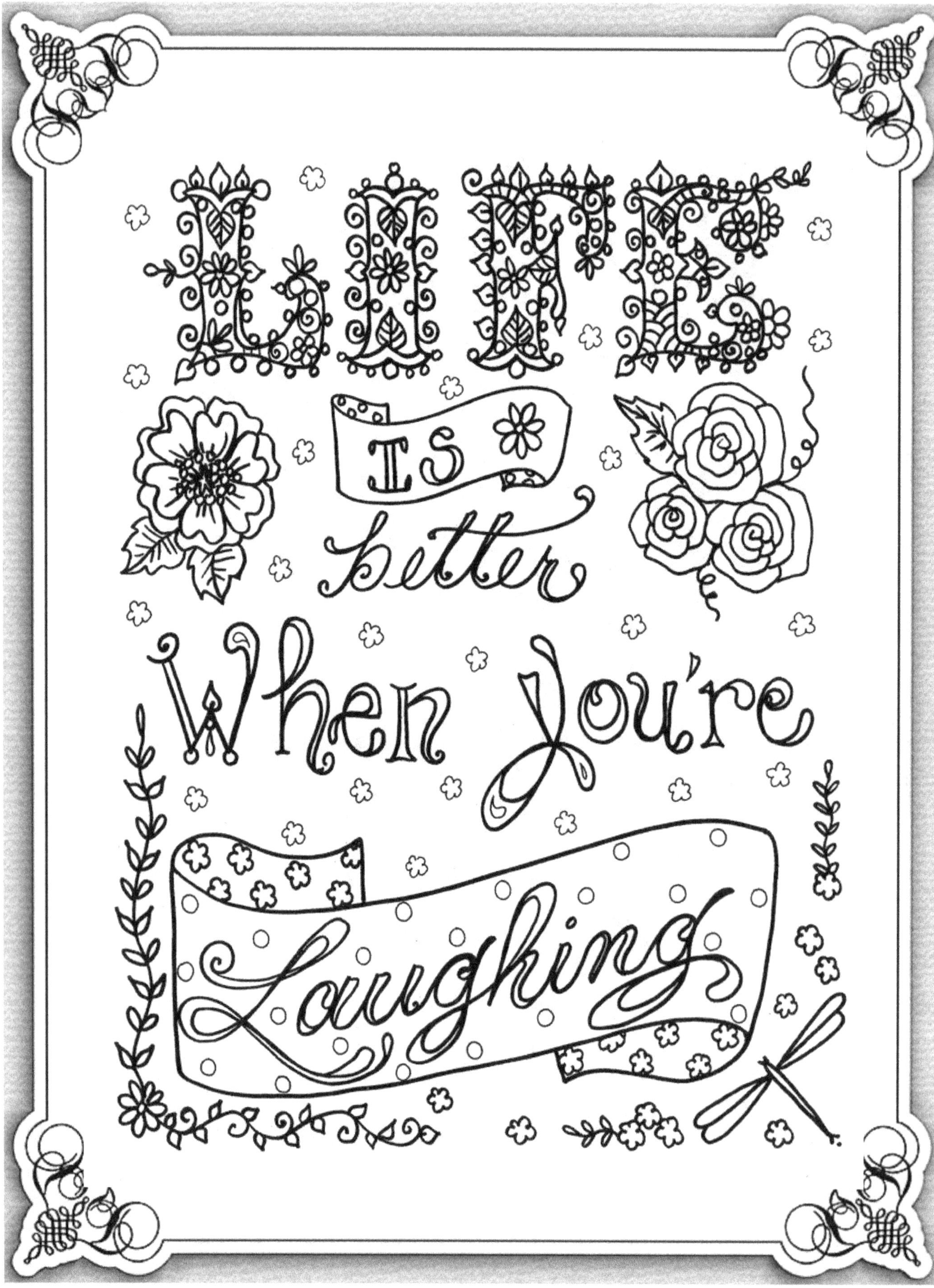
LIFE
IS
better
When You're
Laughing

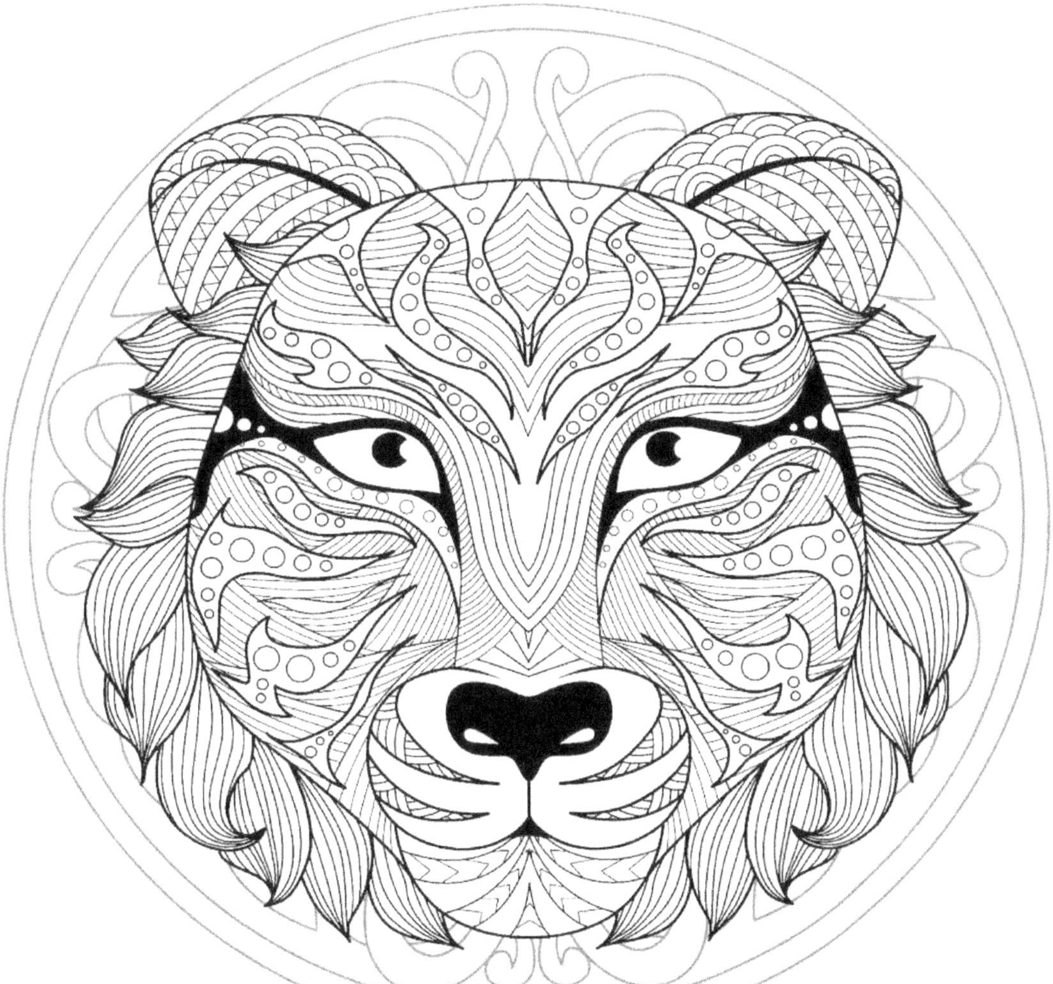

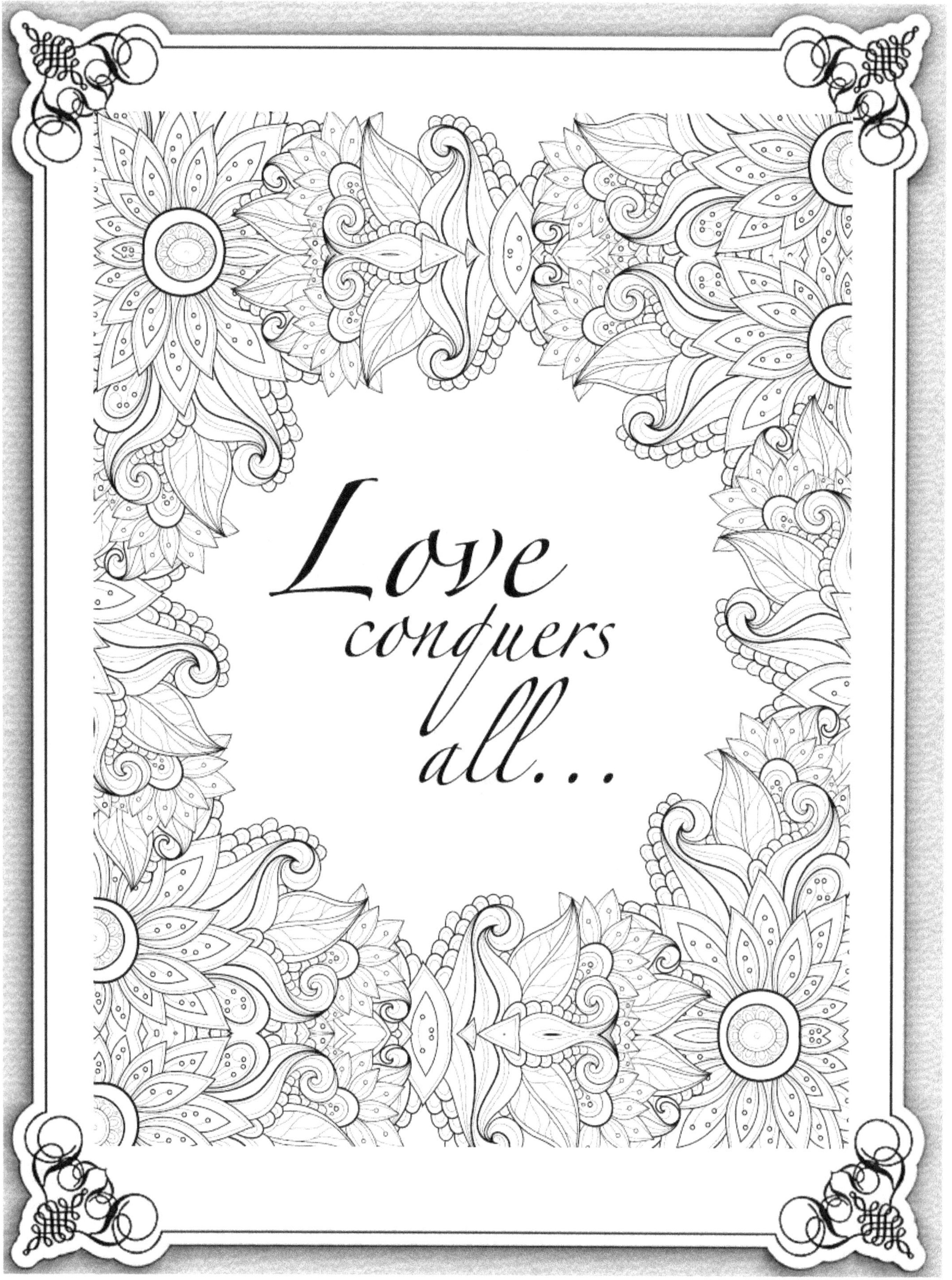
Love conquers all...

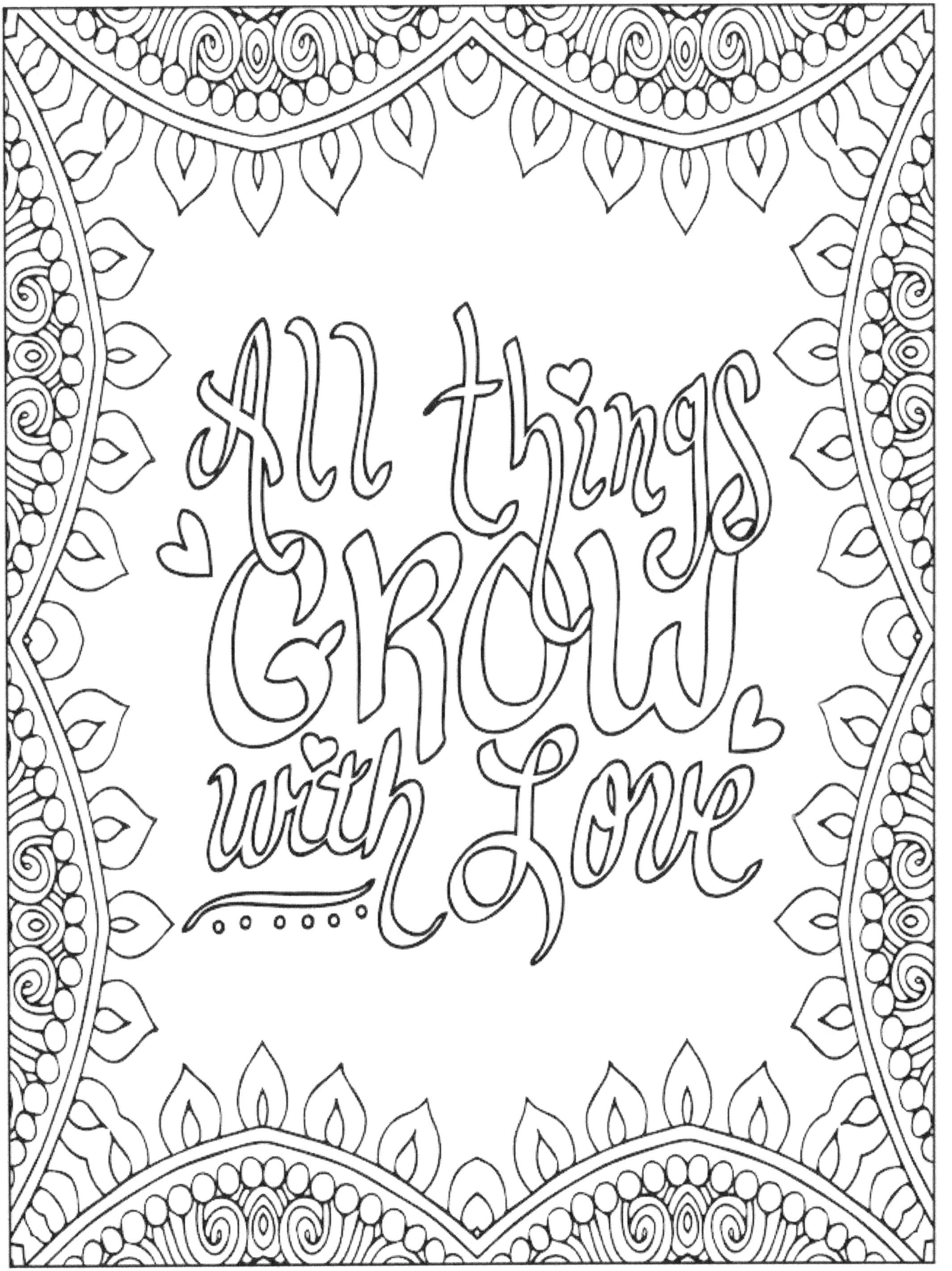
All things
GROW
with Love

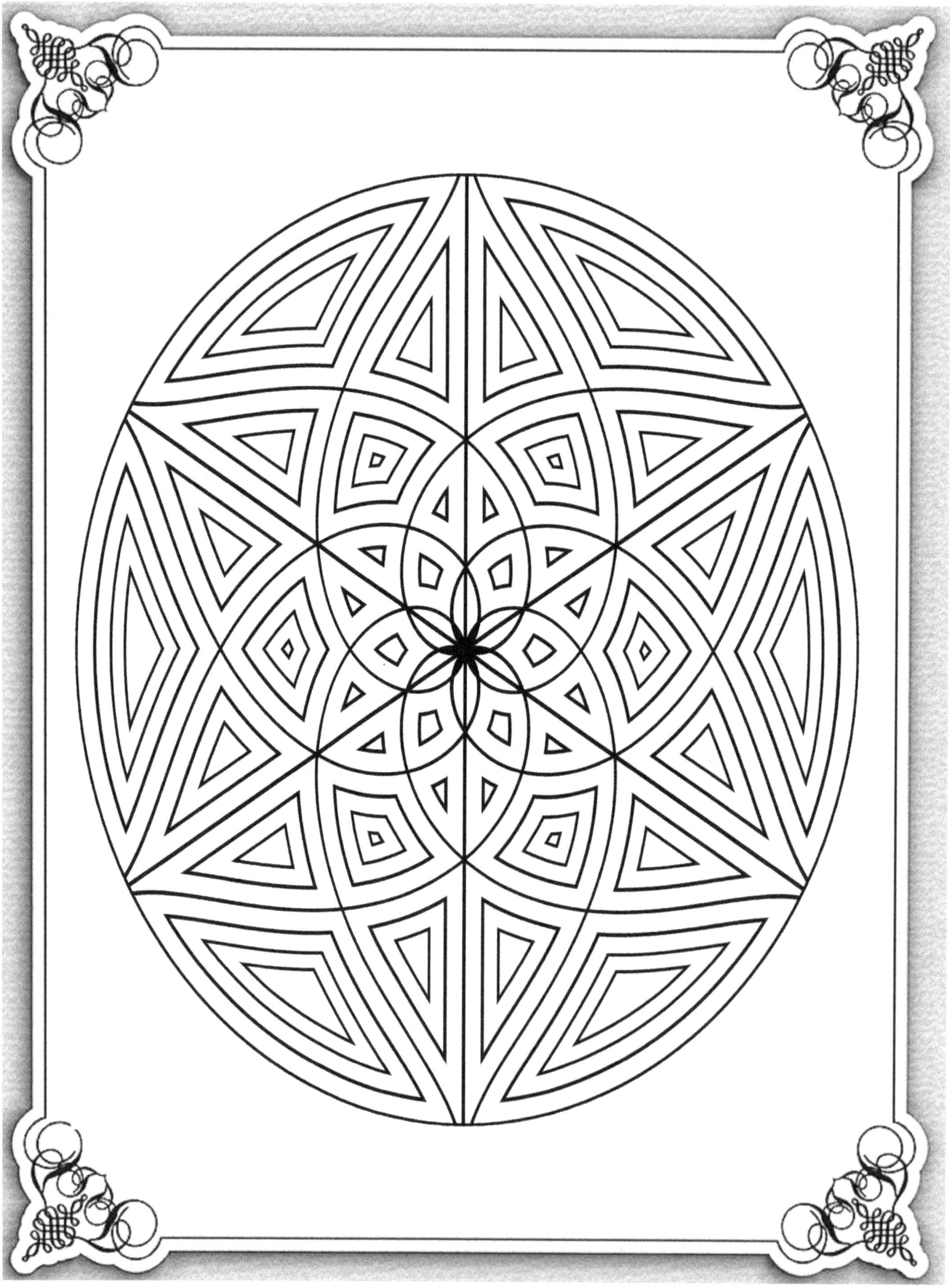

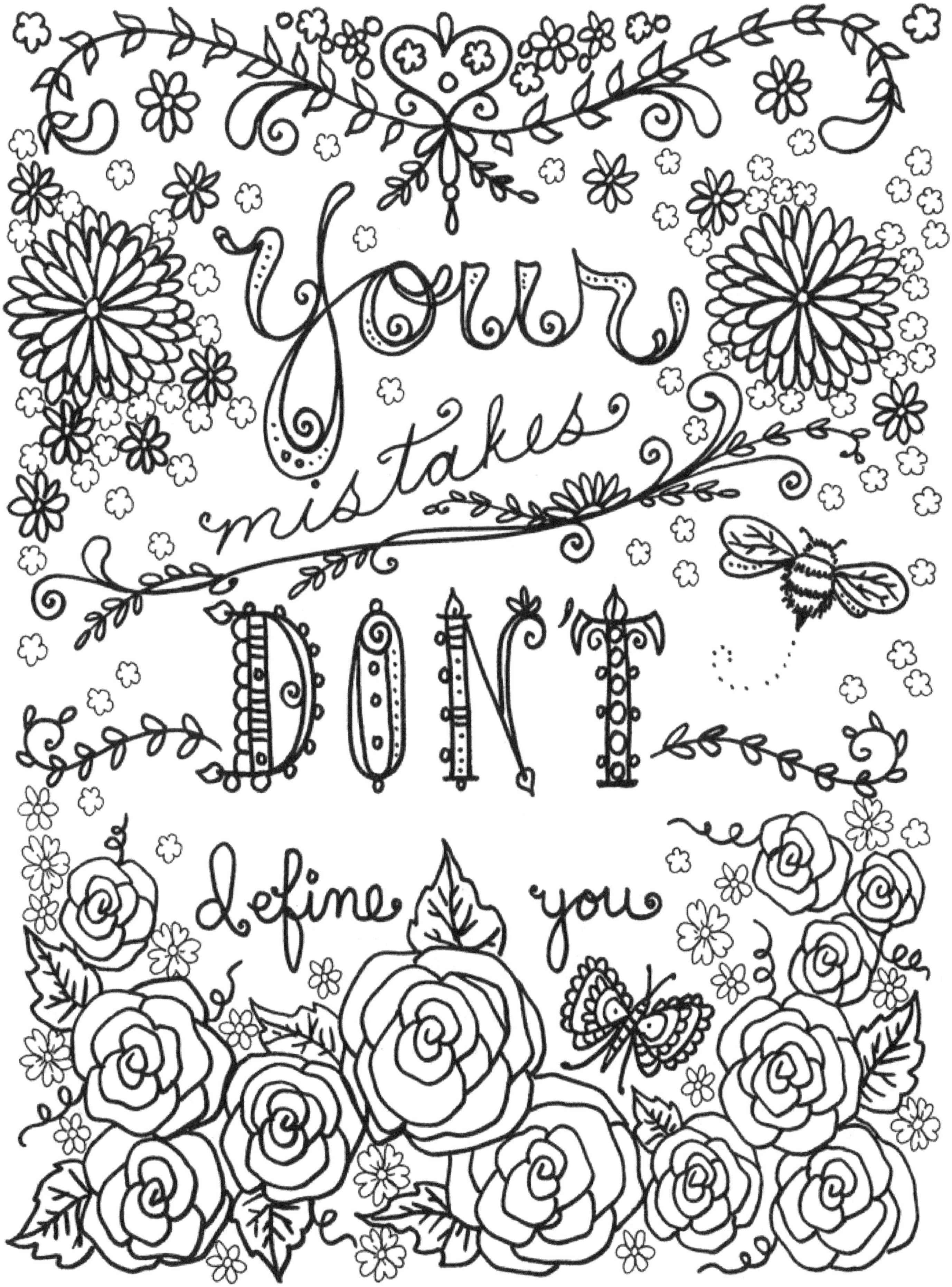
Your
mistakes
DON'T
define you

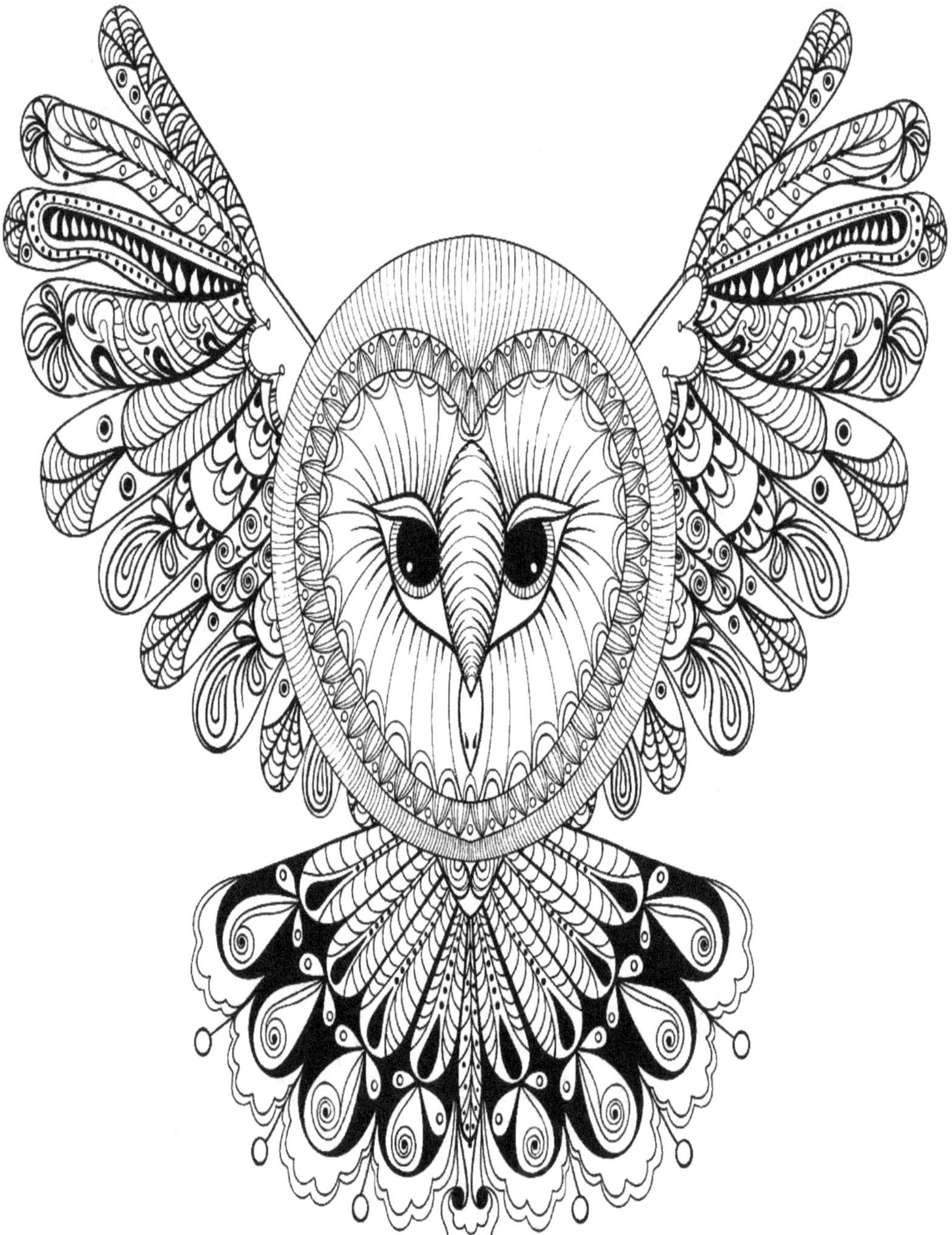

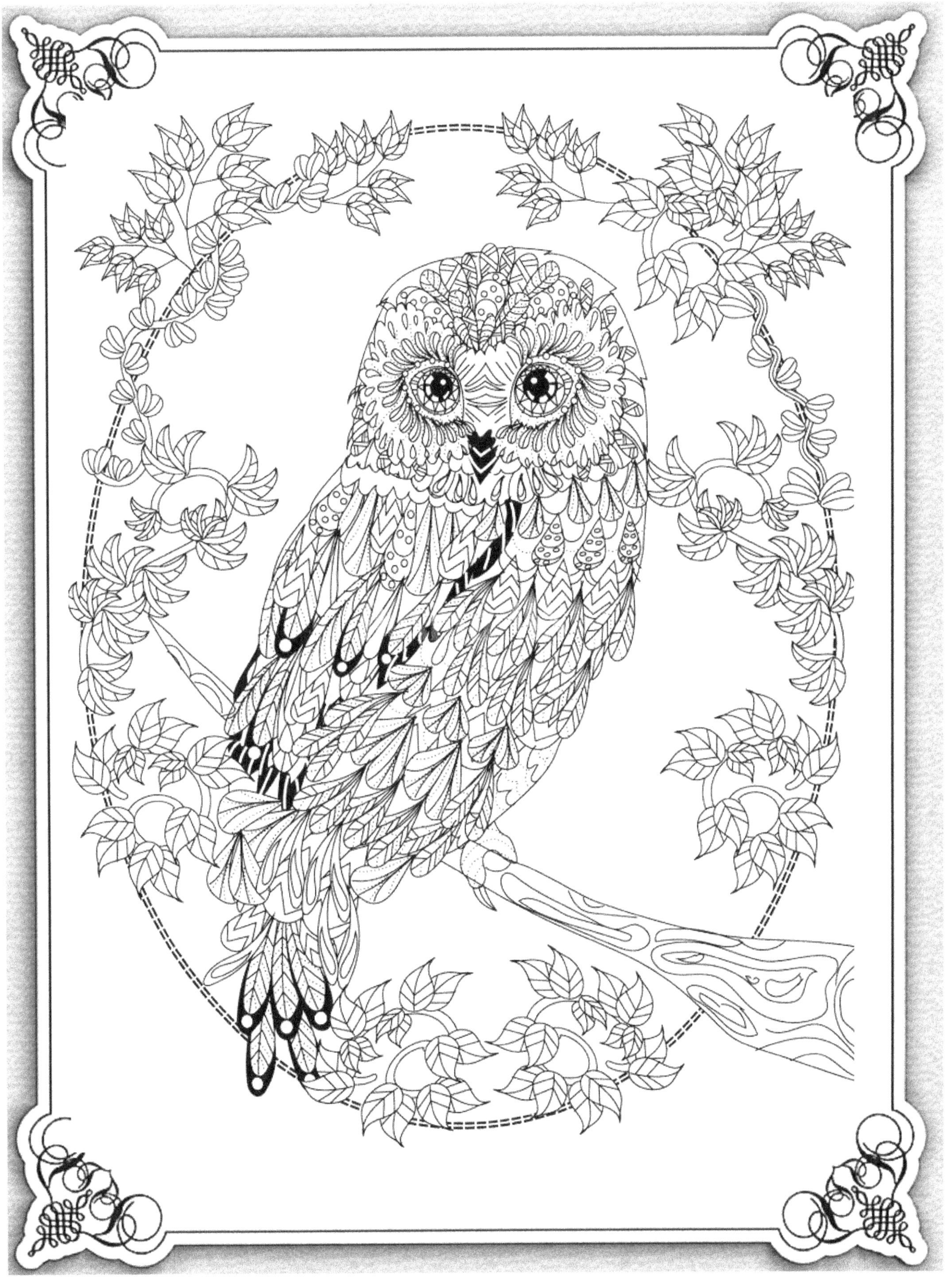

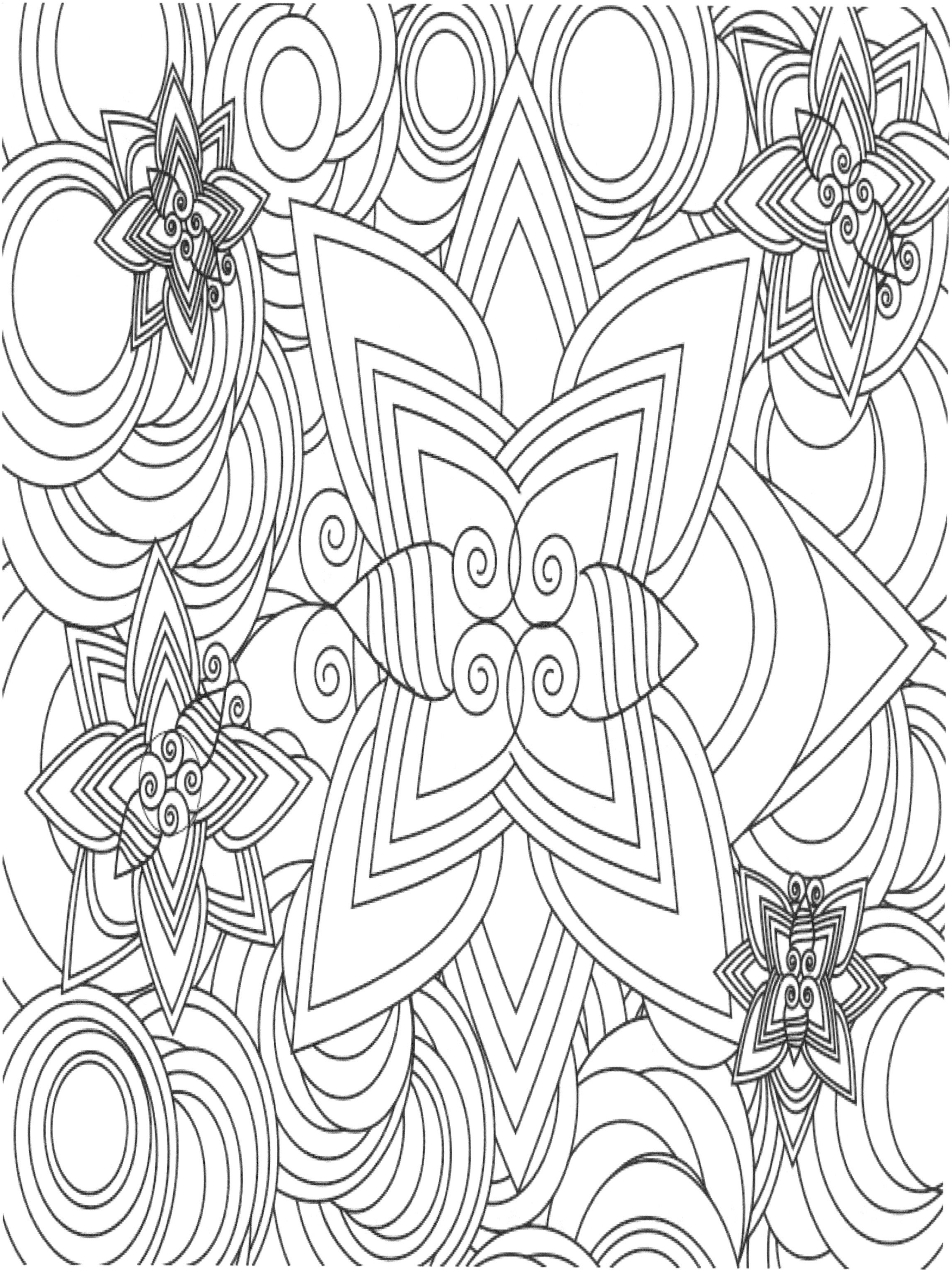

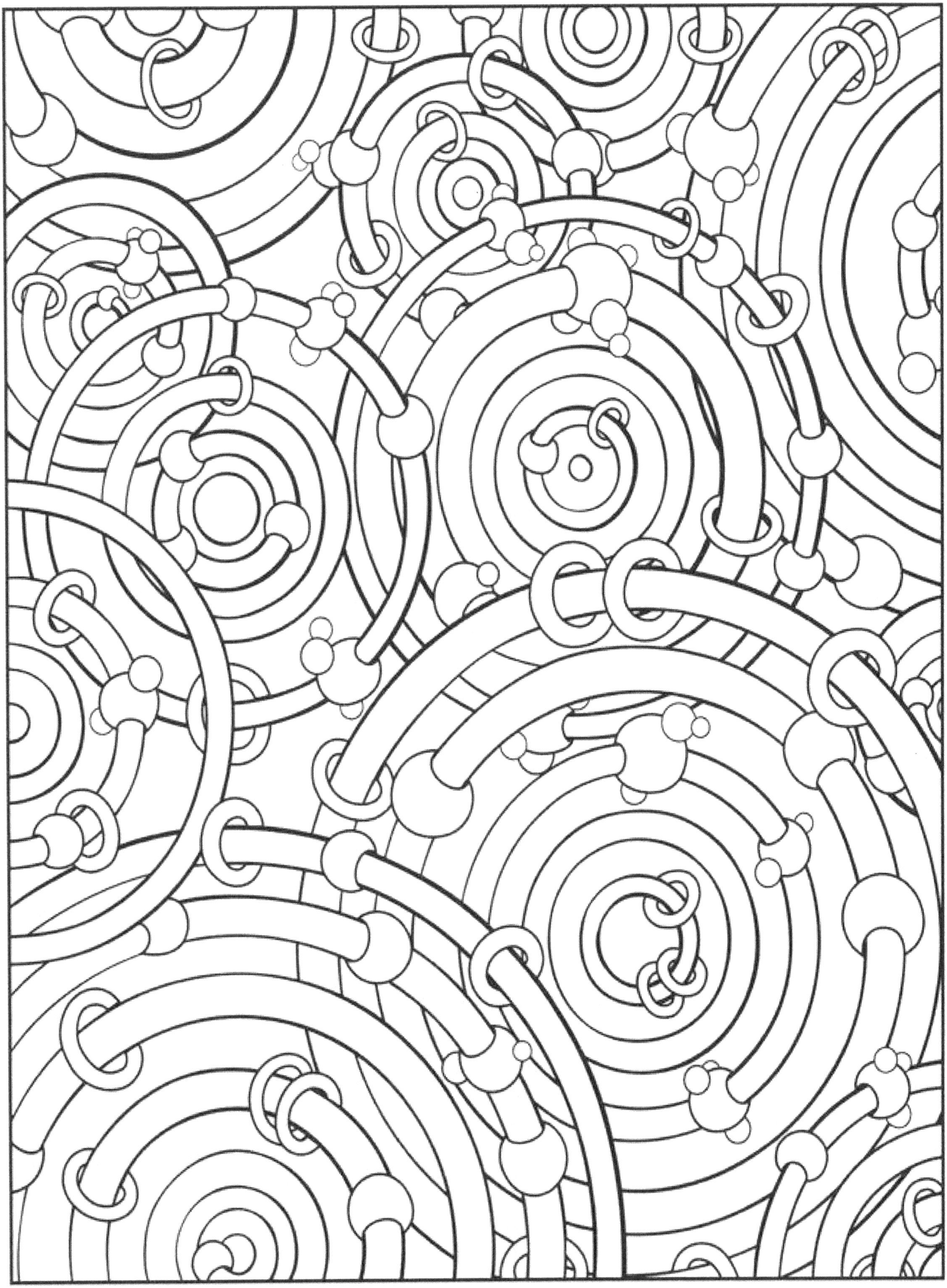

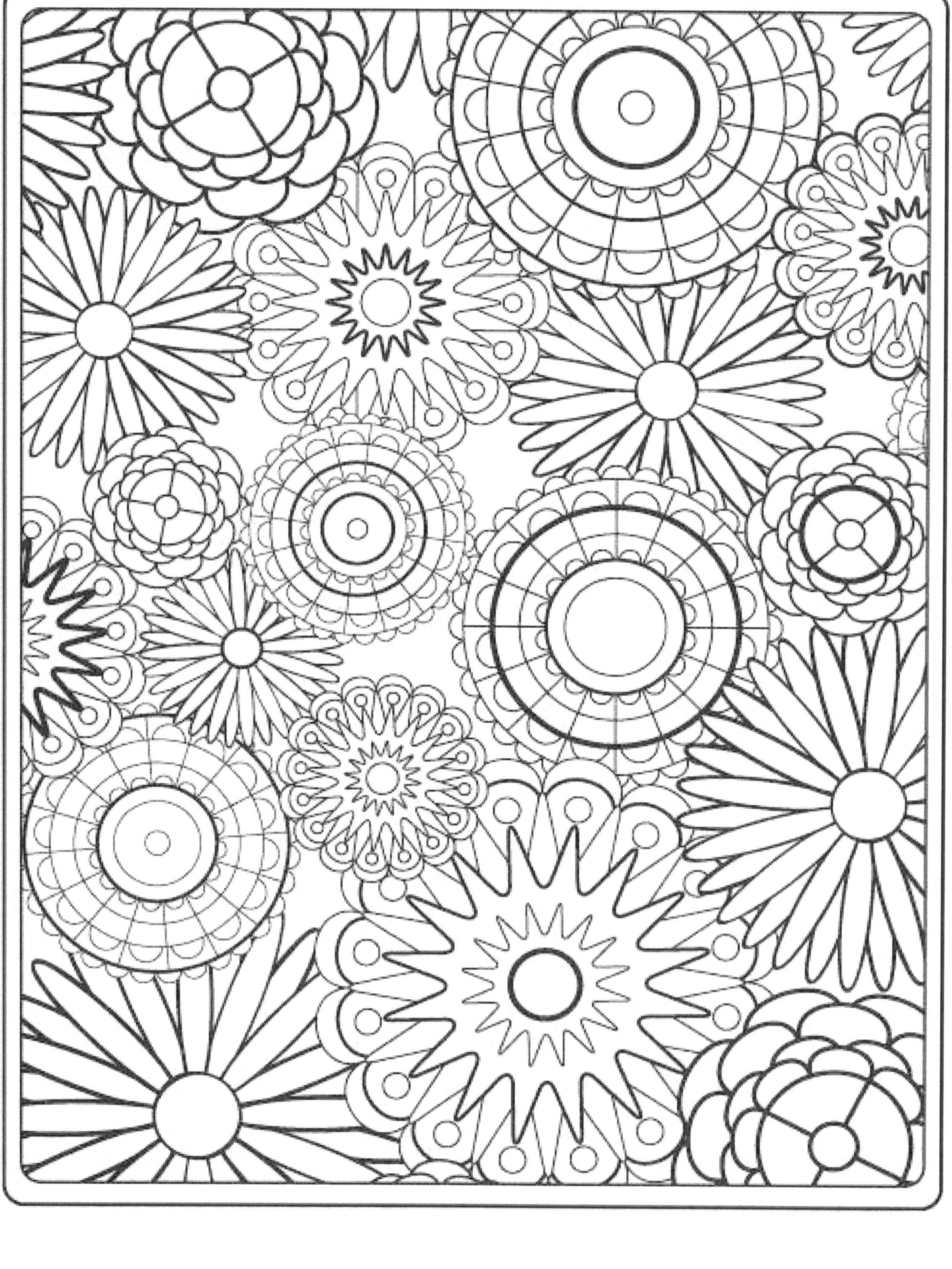

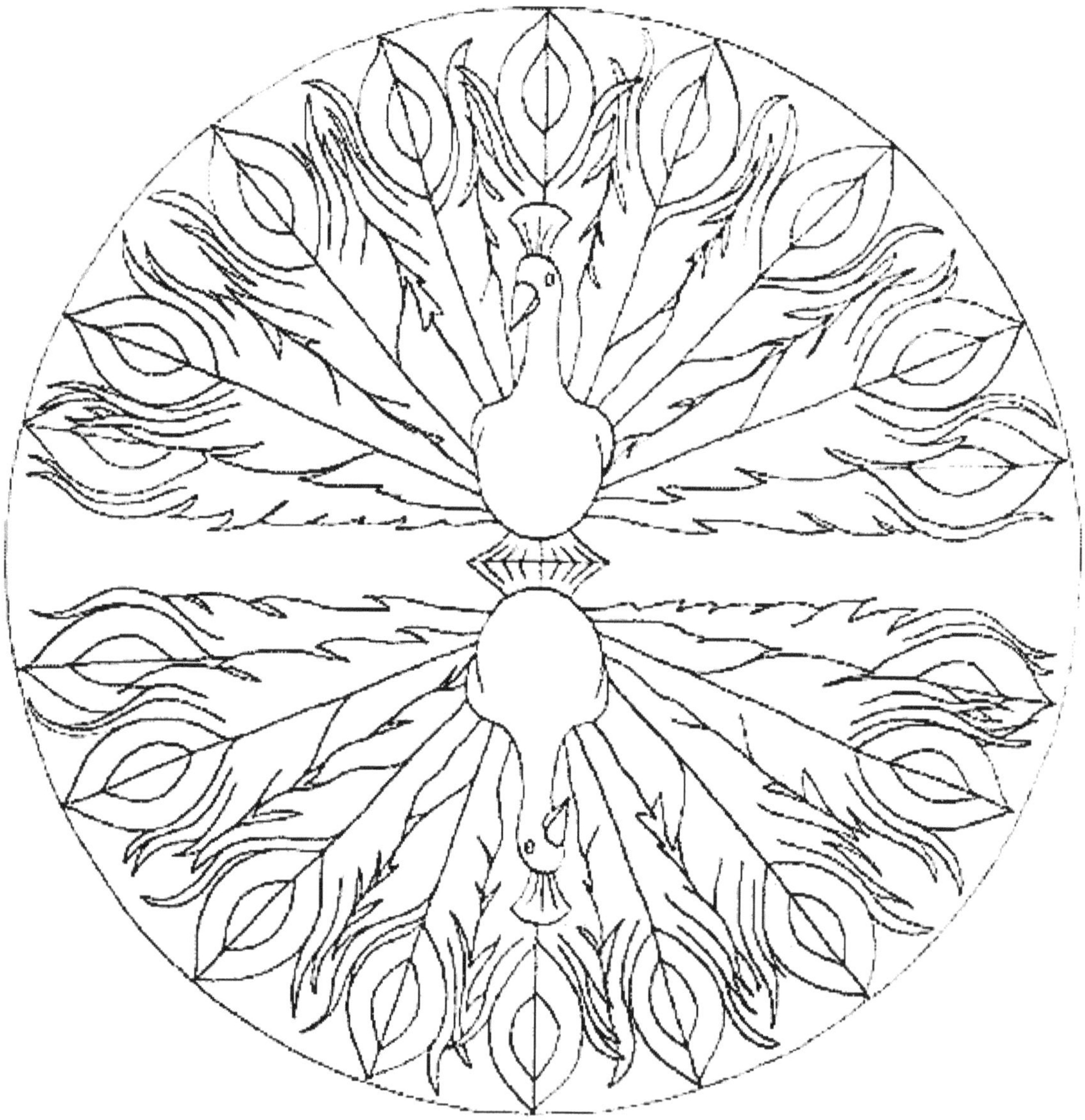

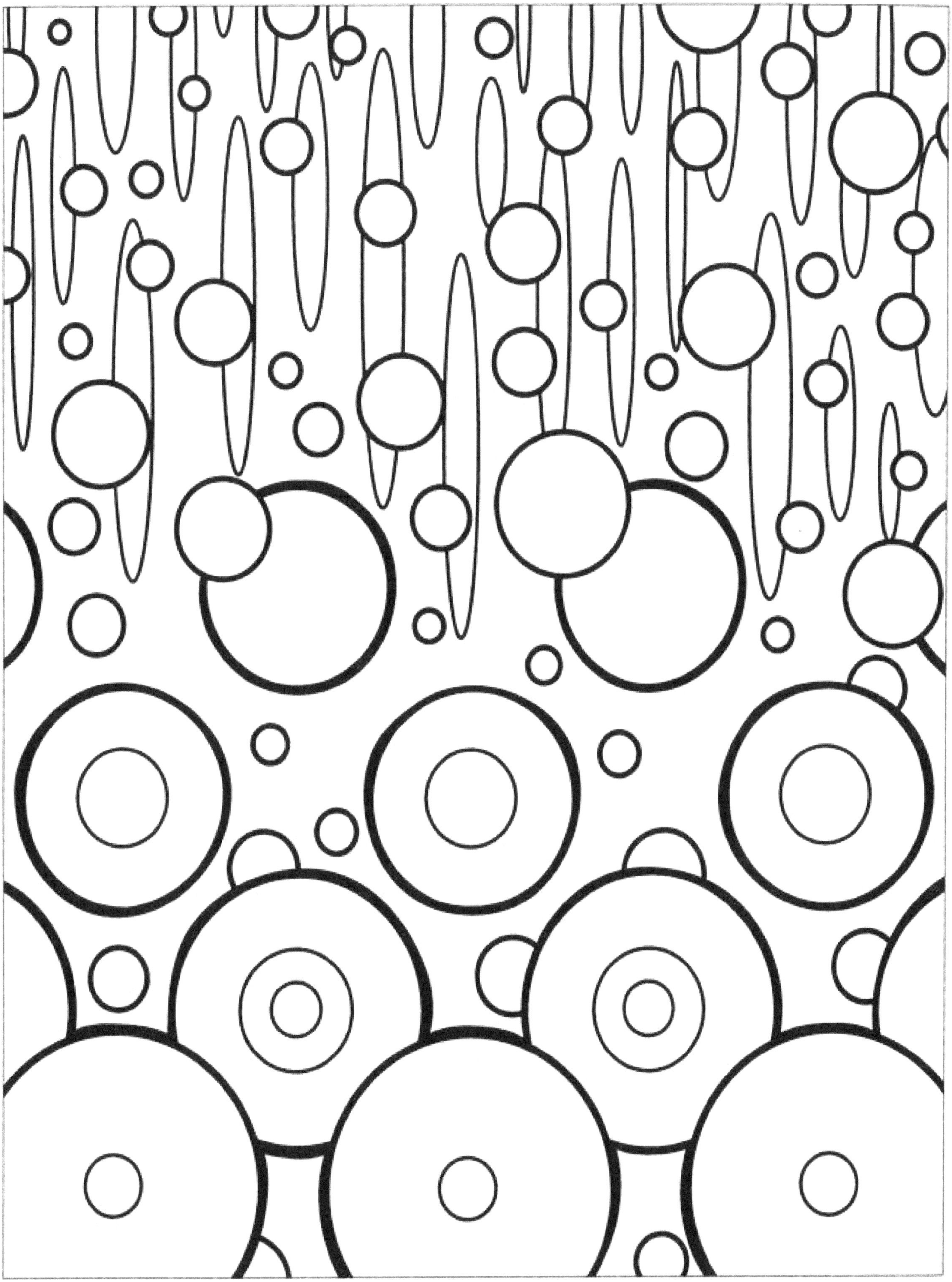

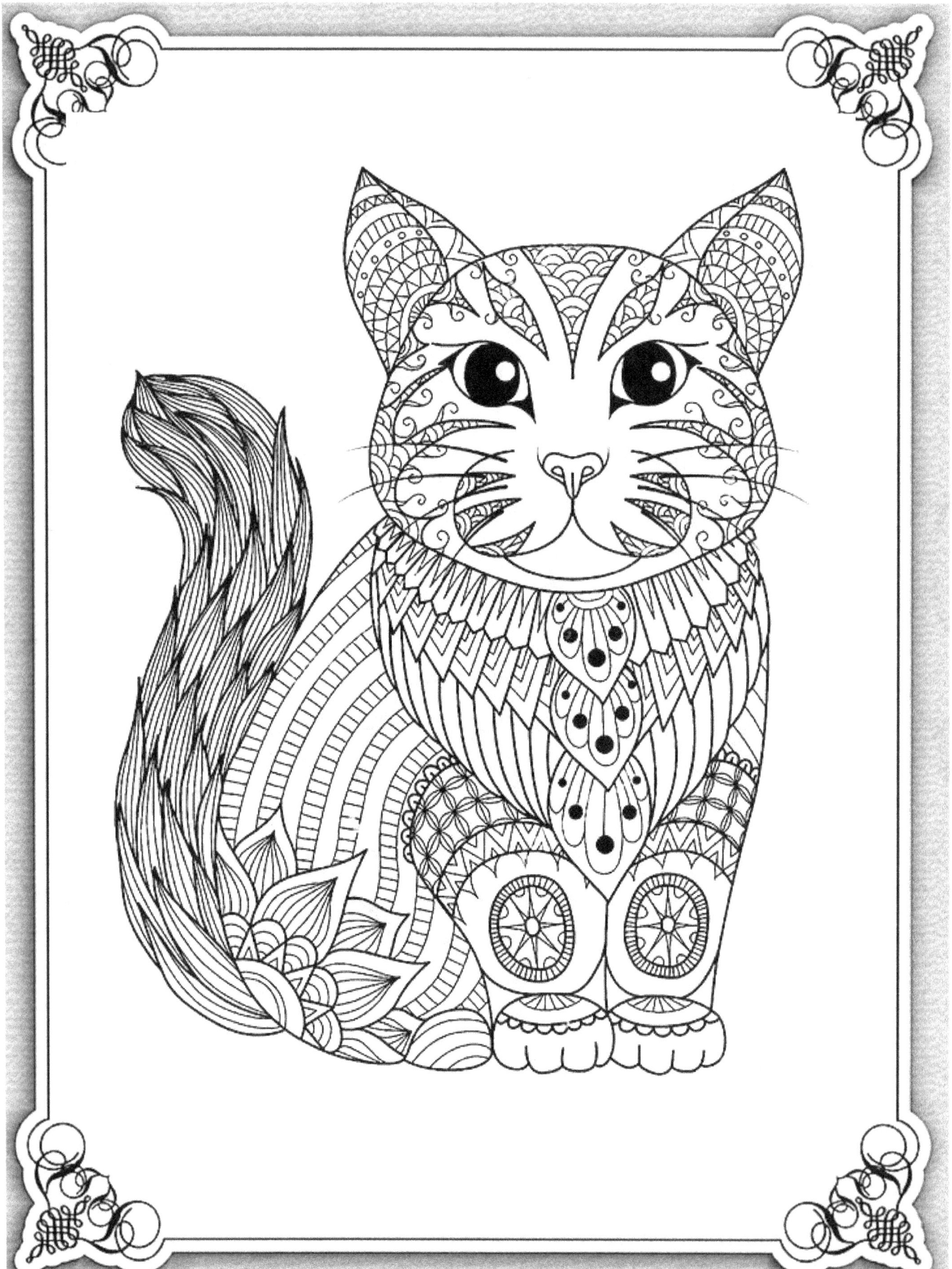

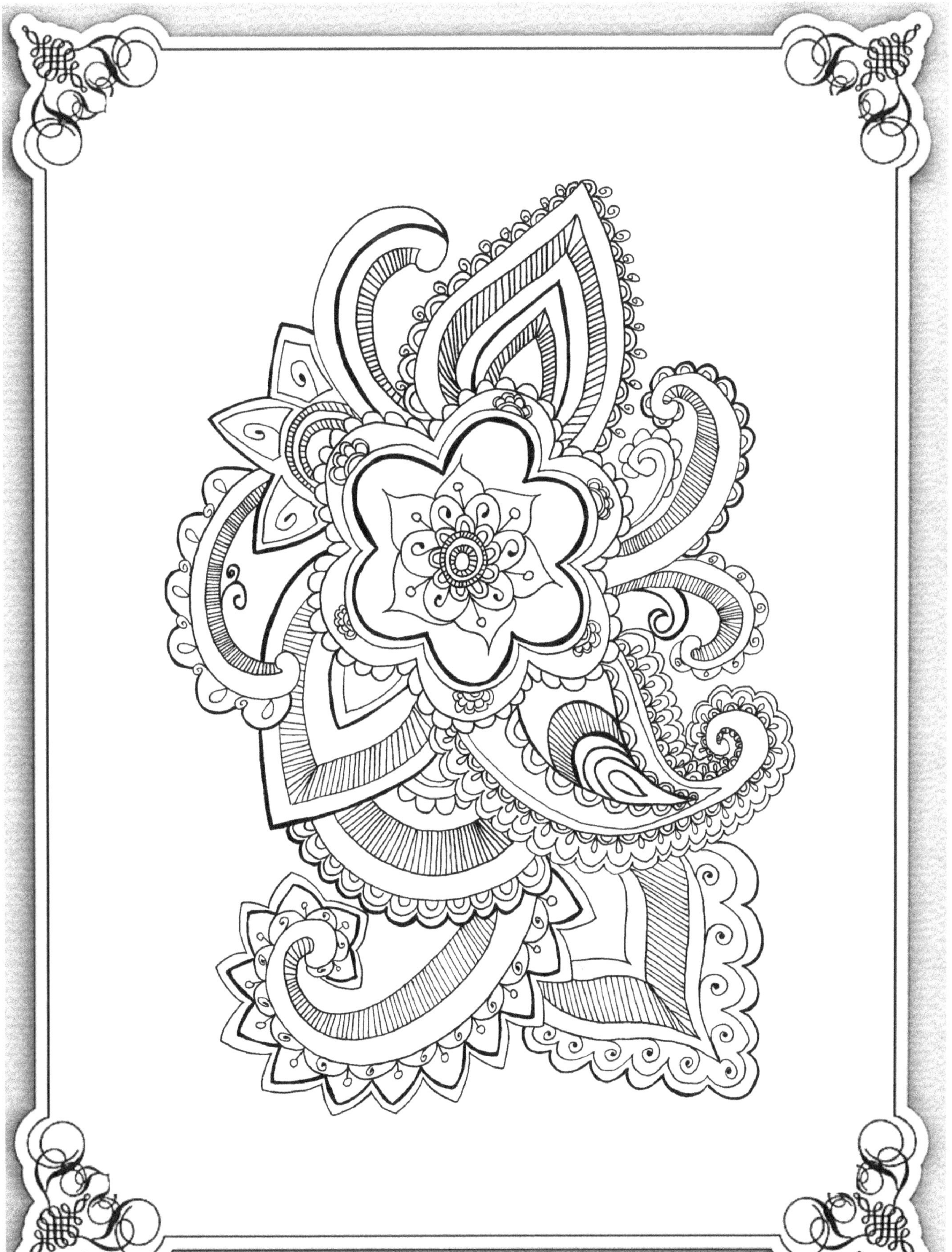

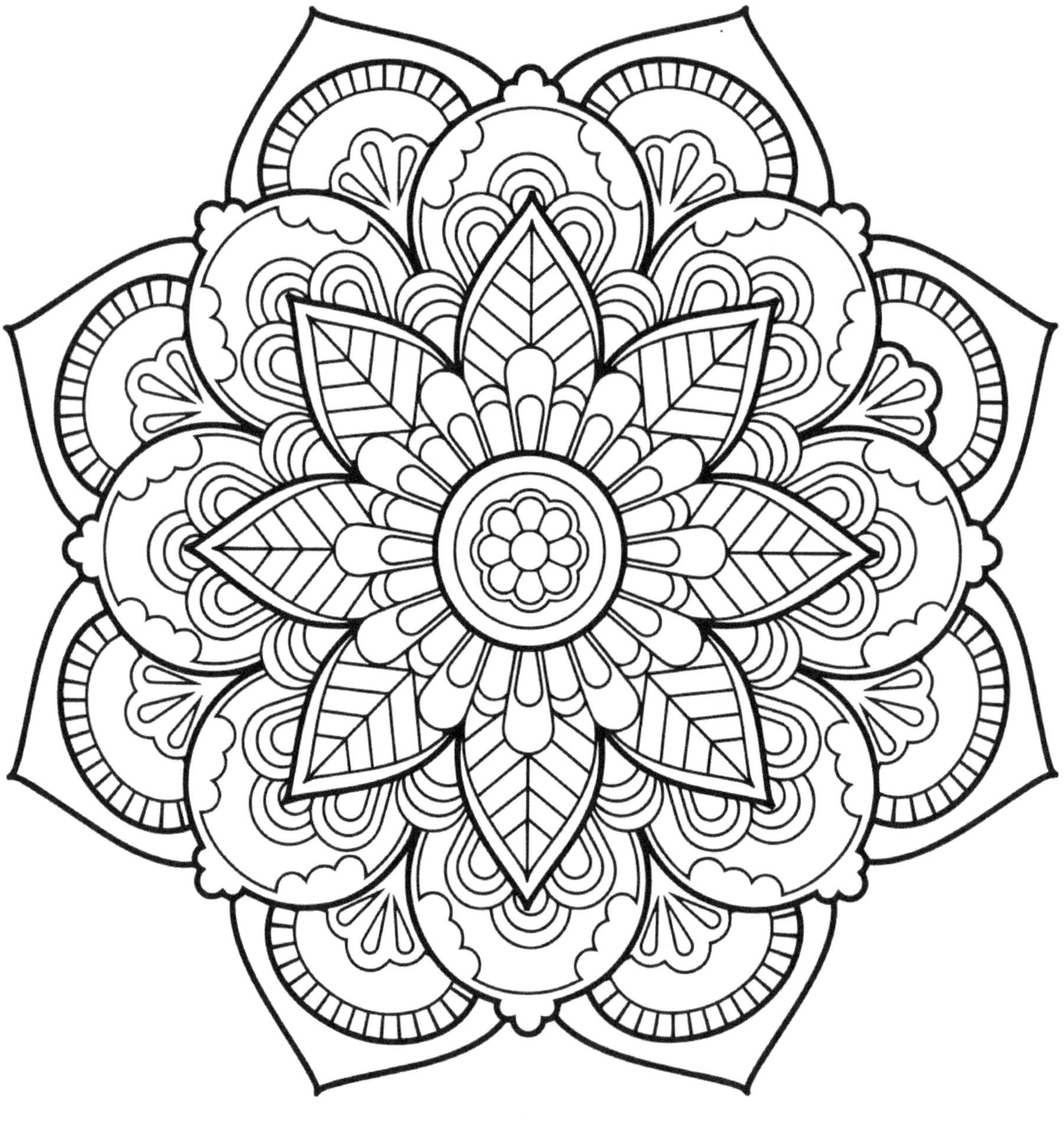

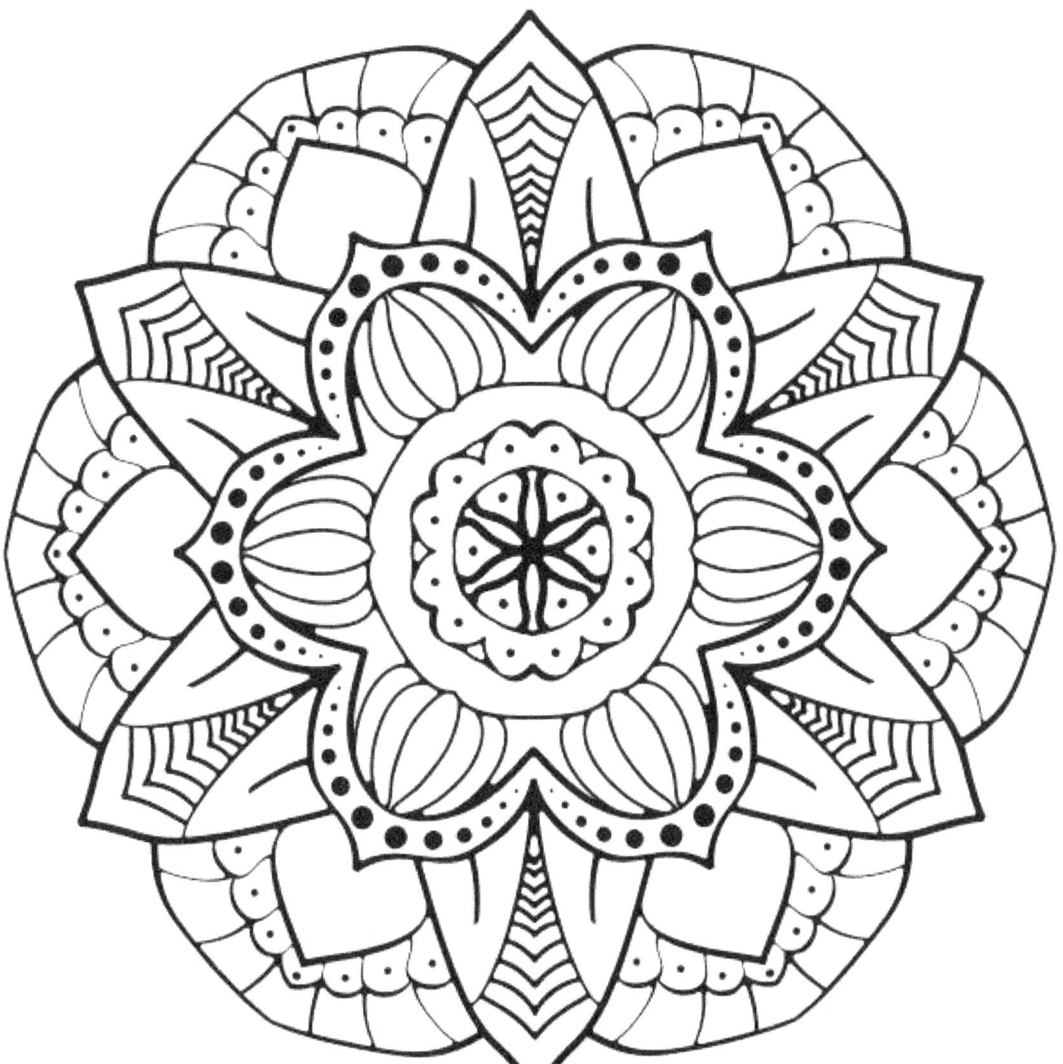

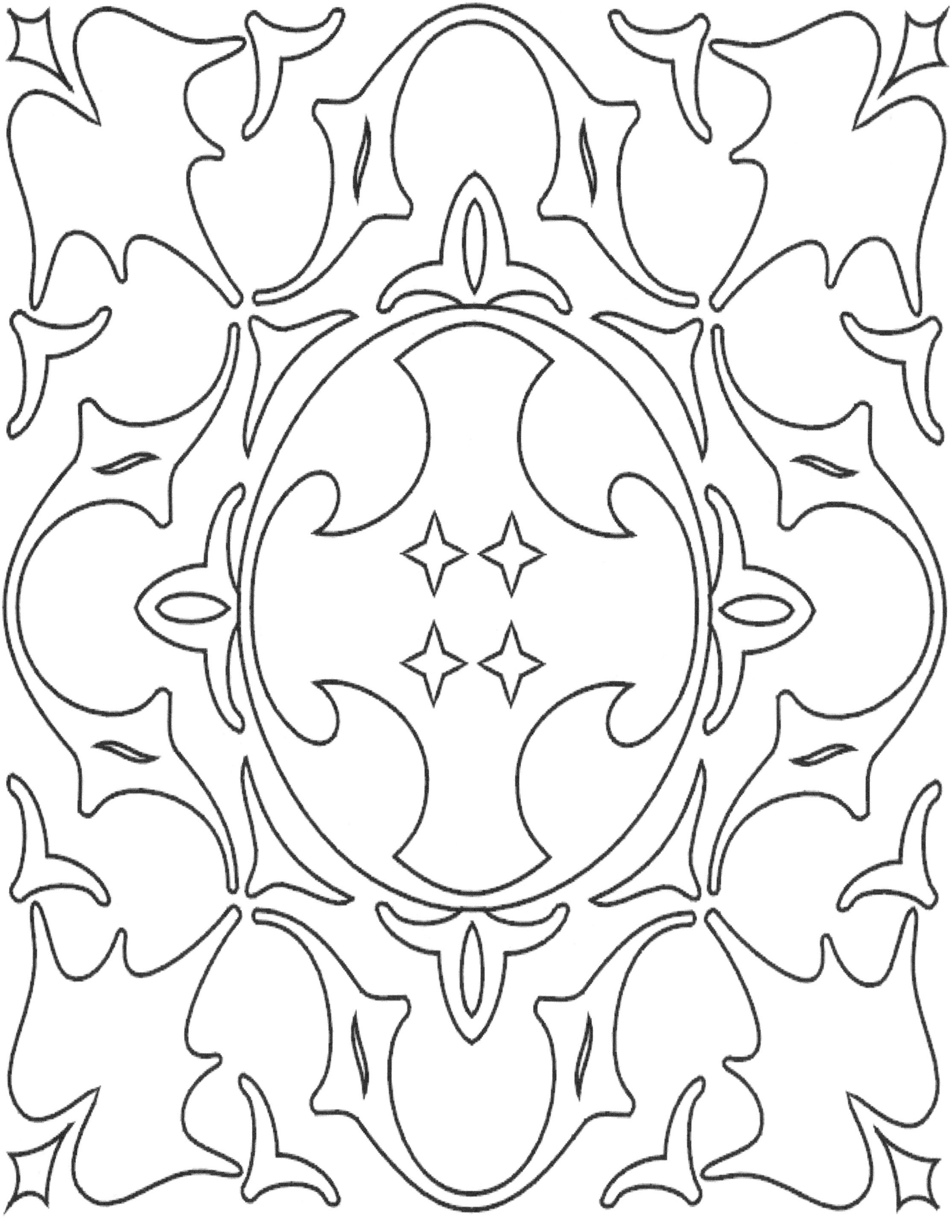

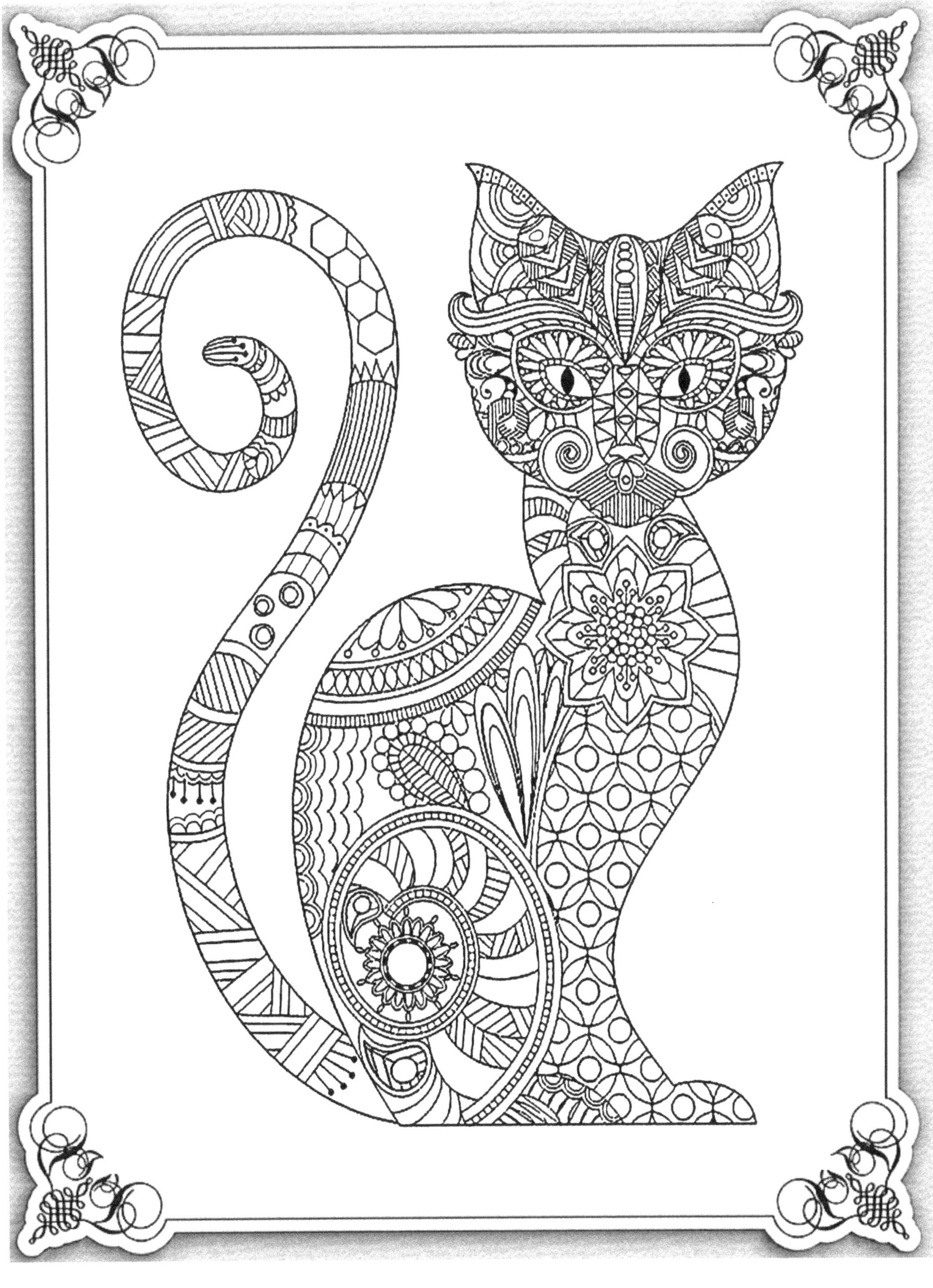

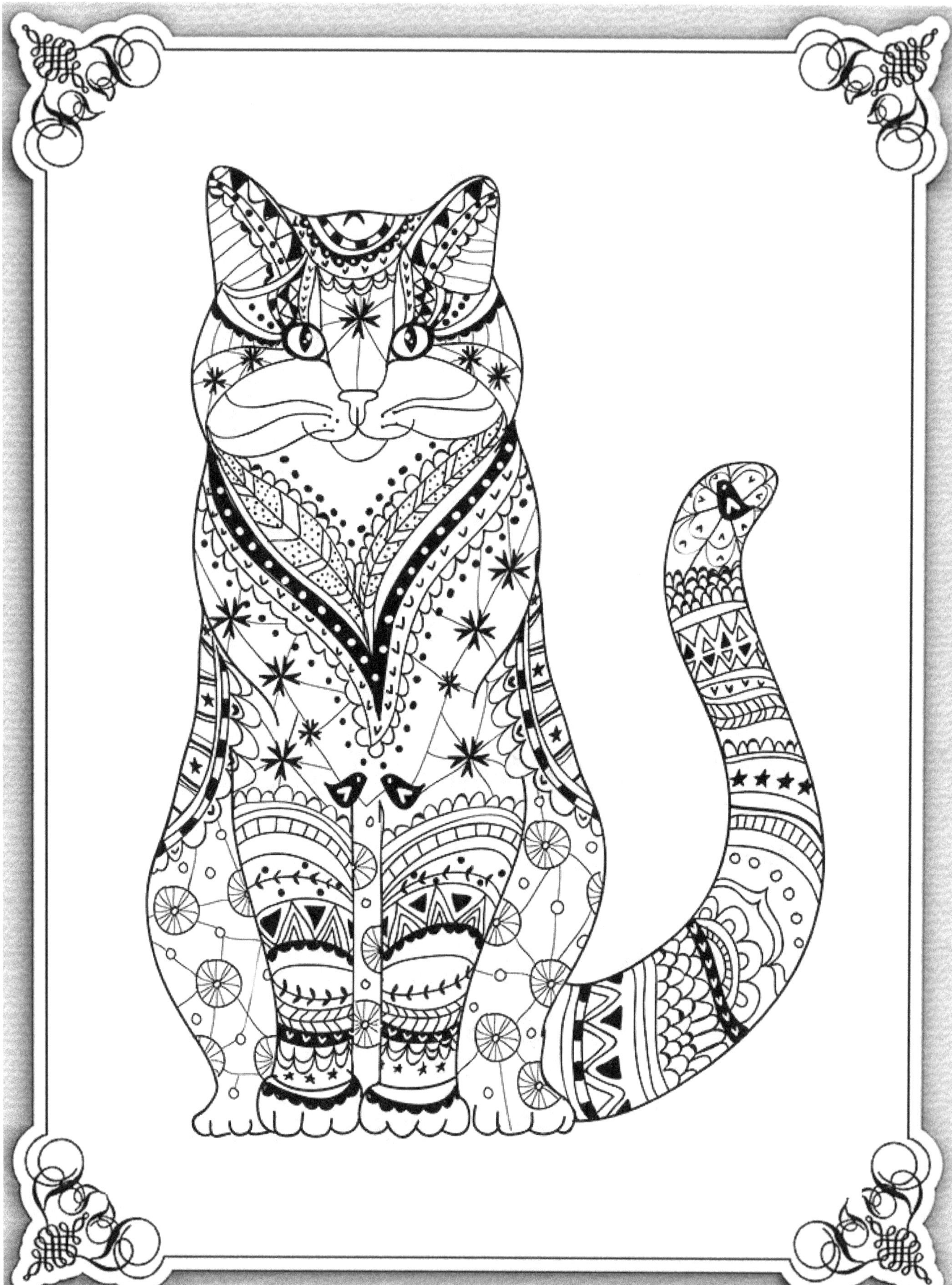

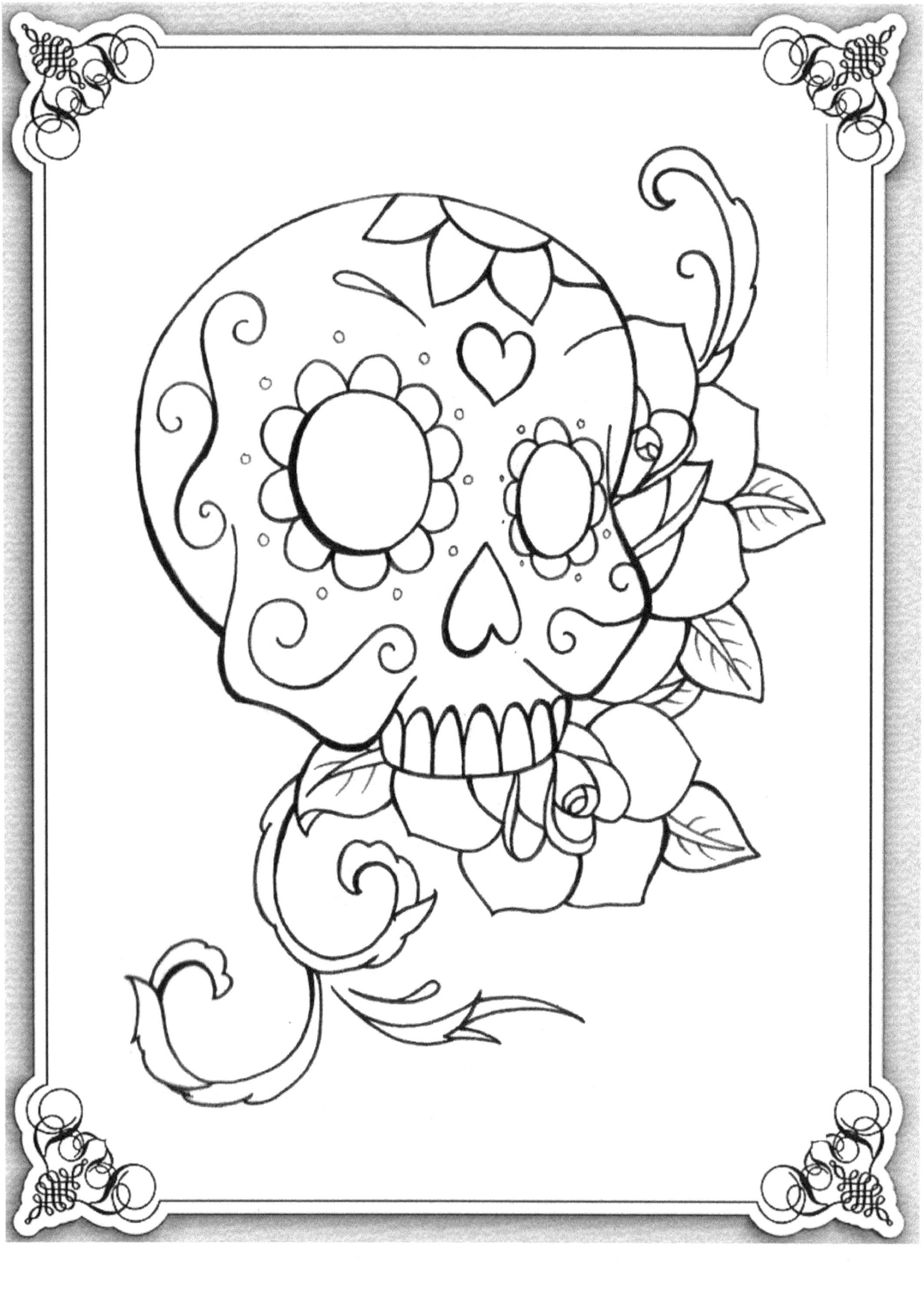

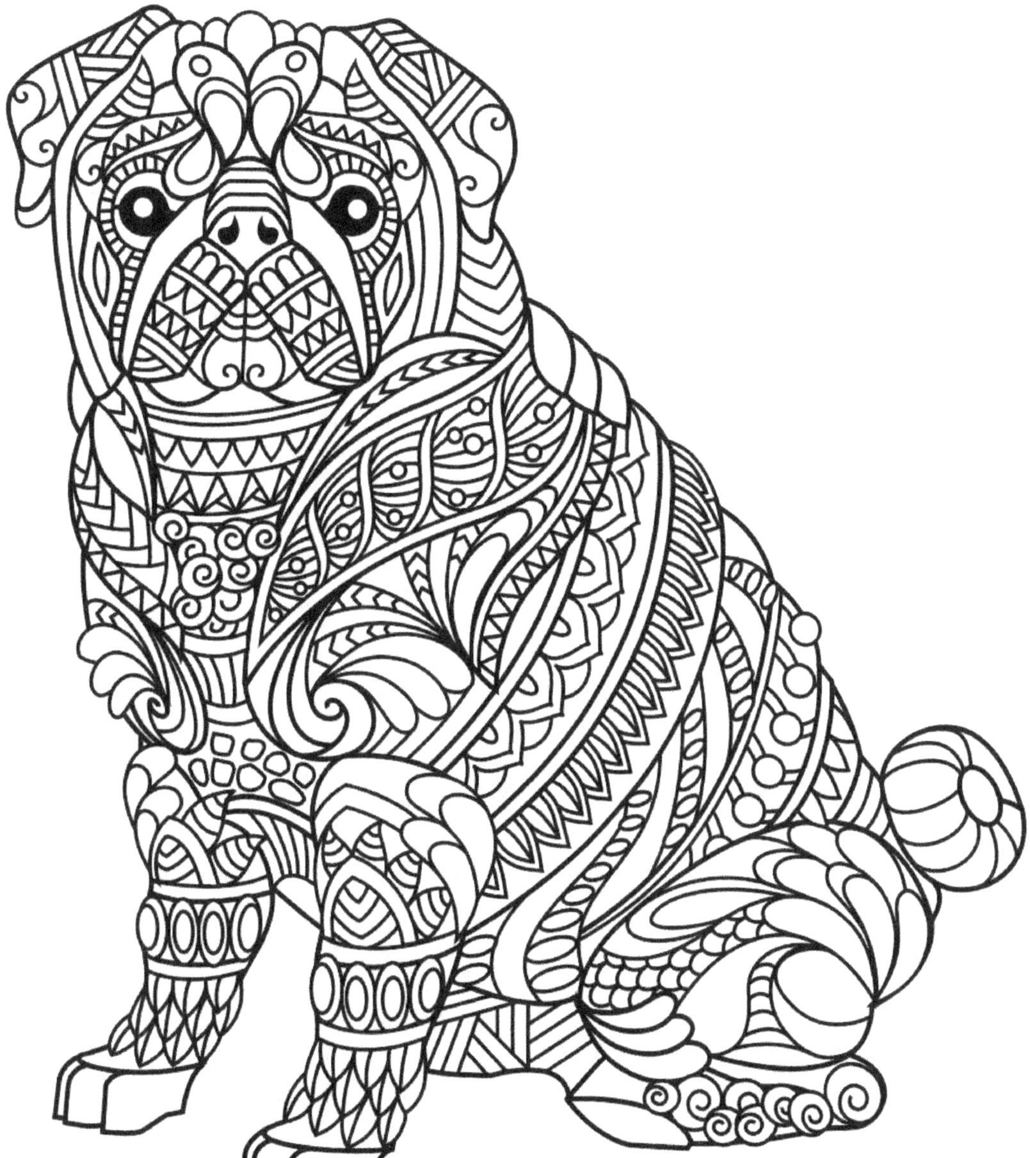

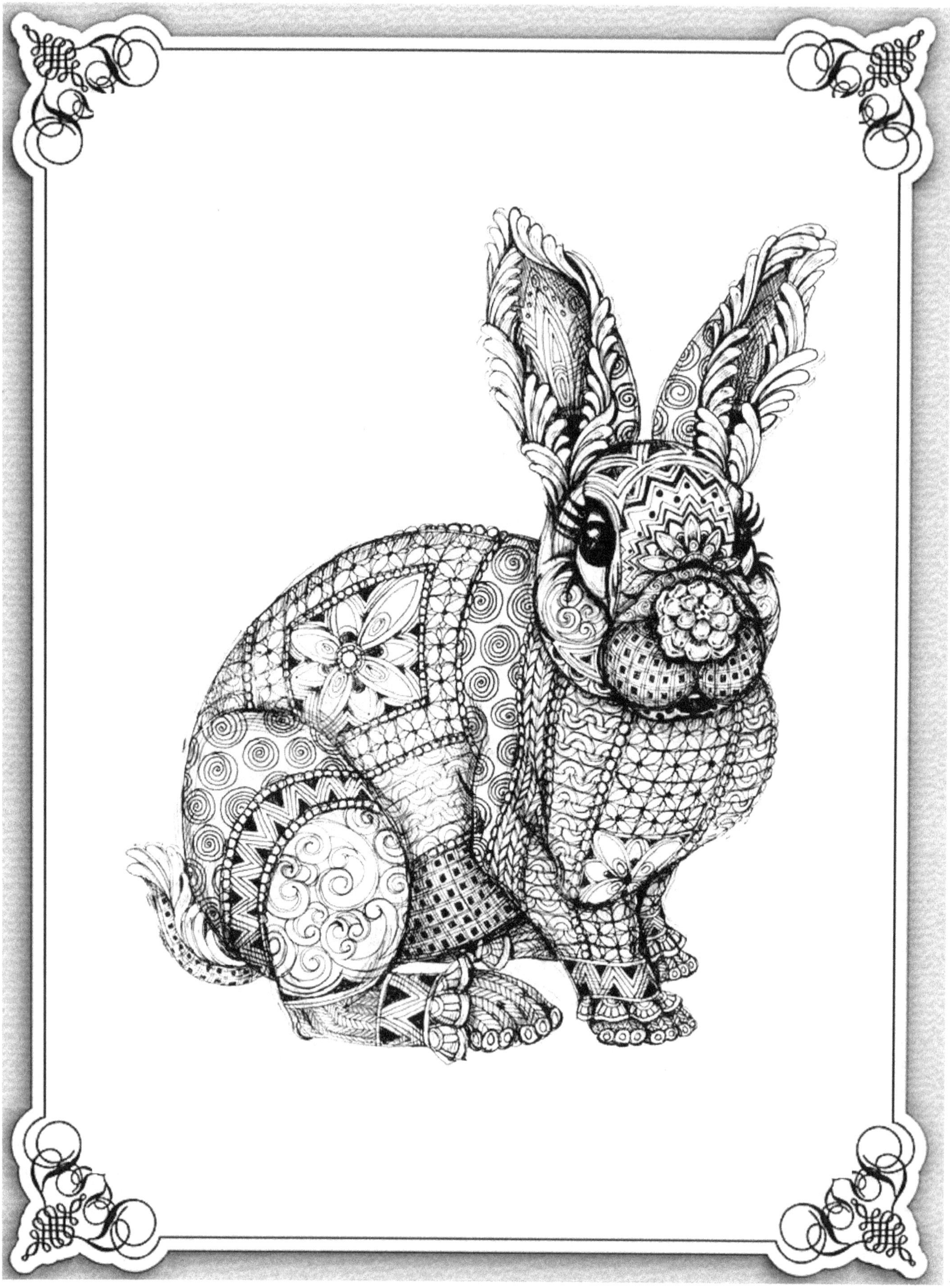

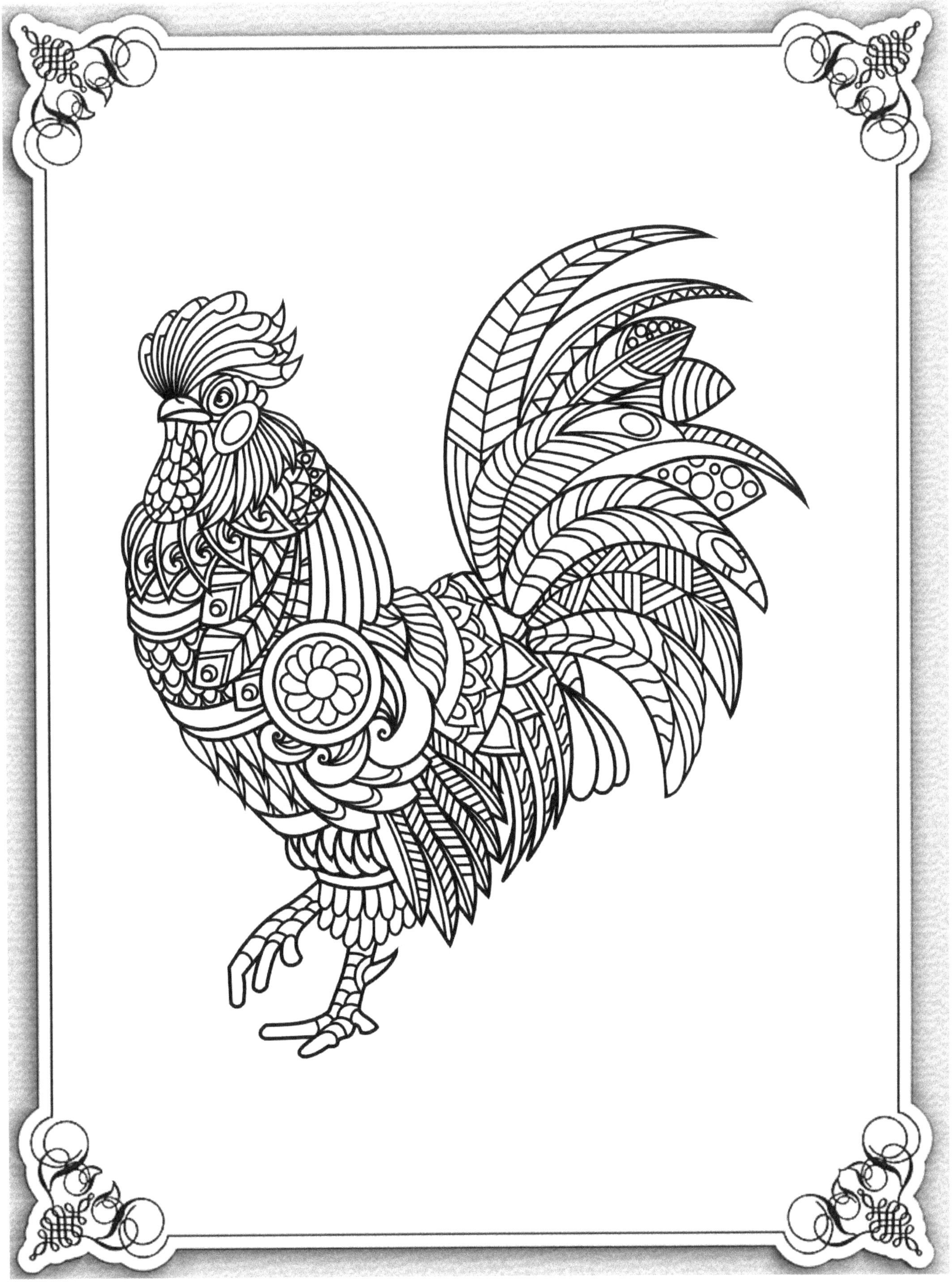

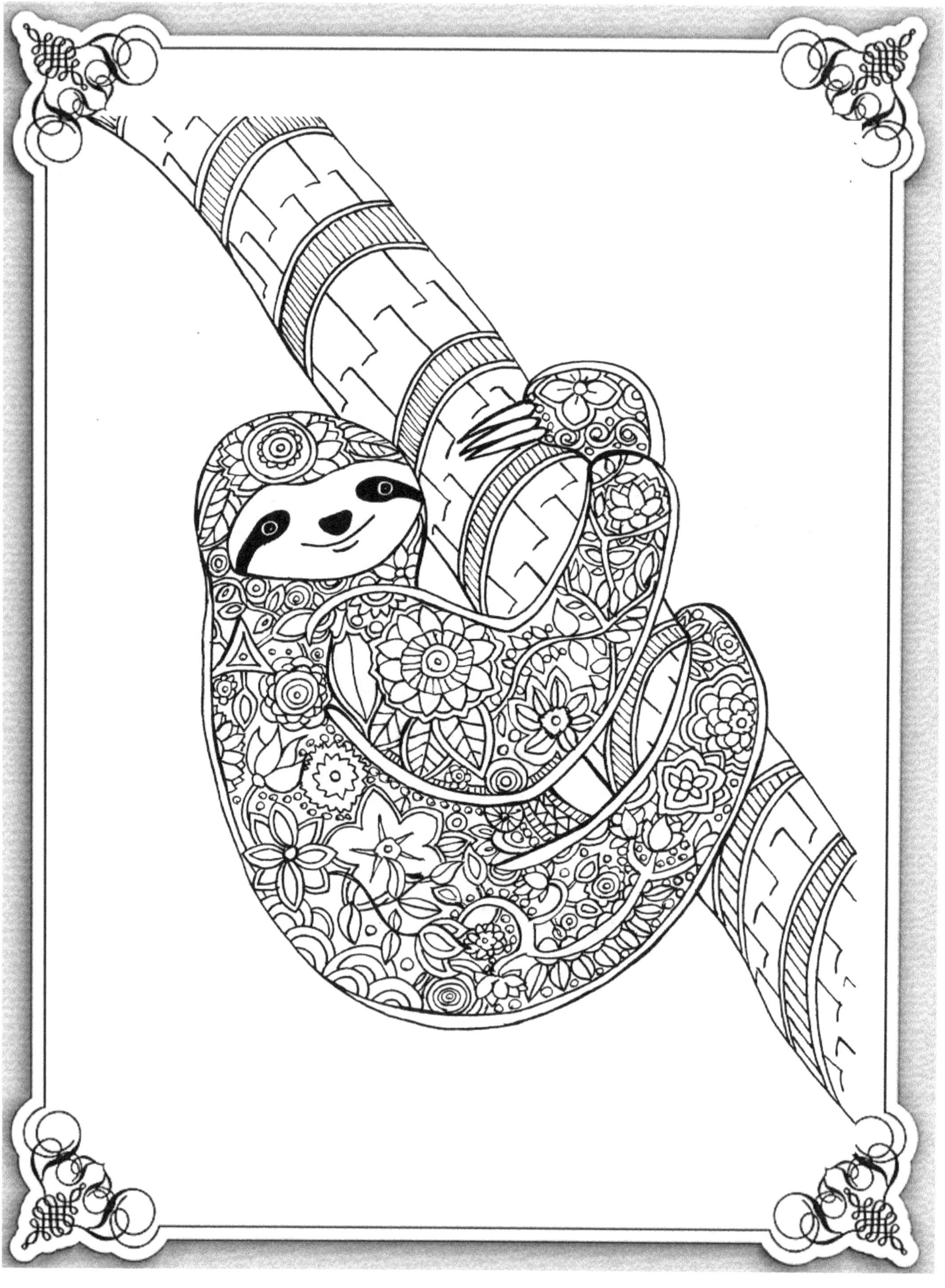

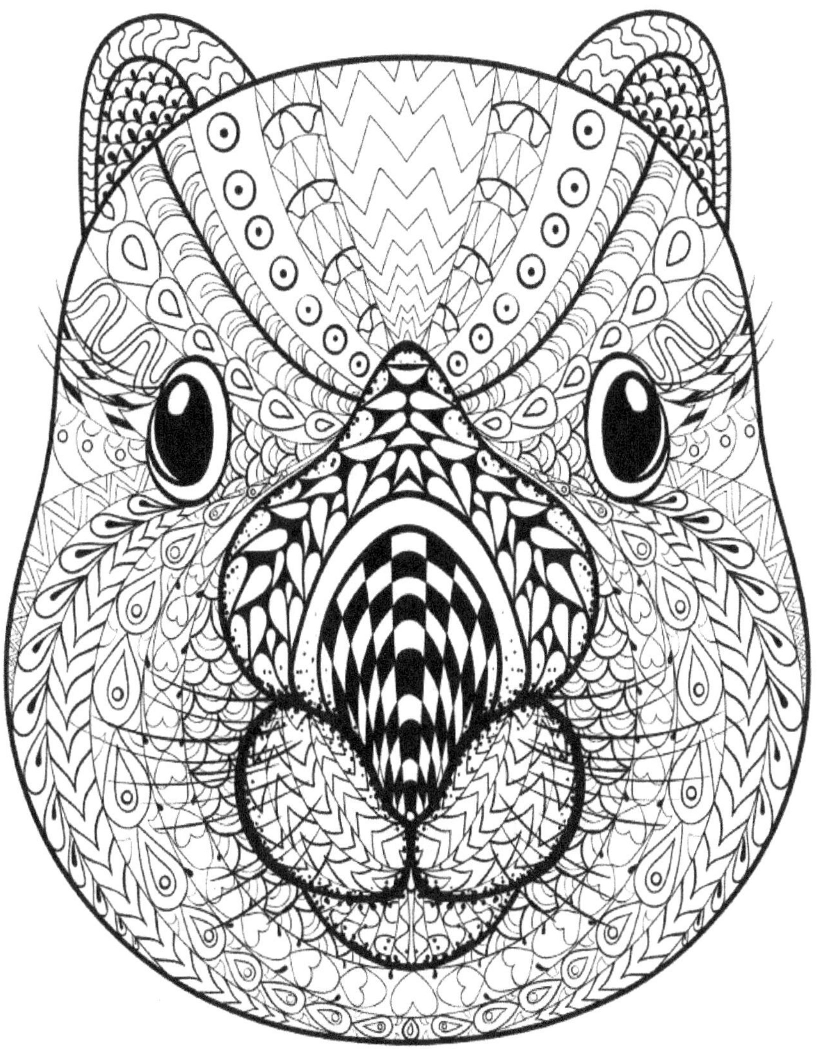

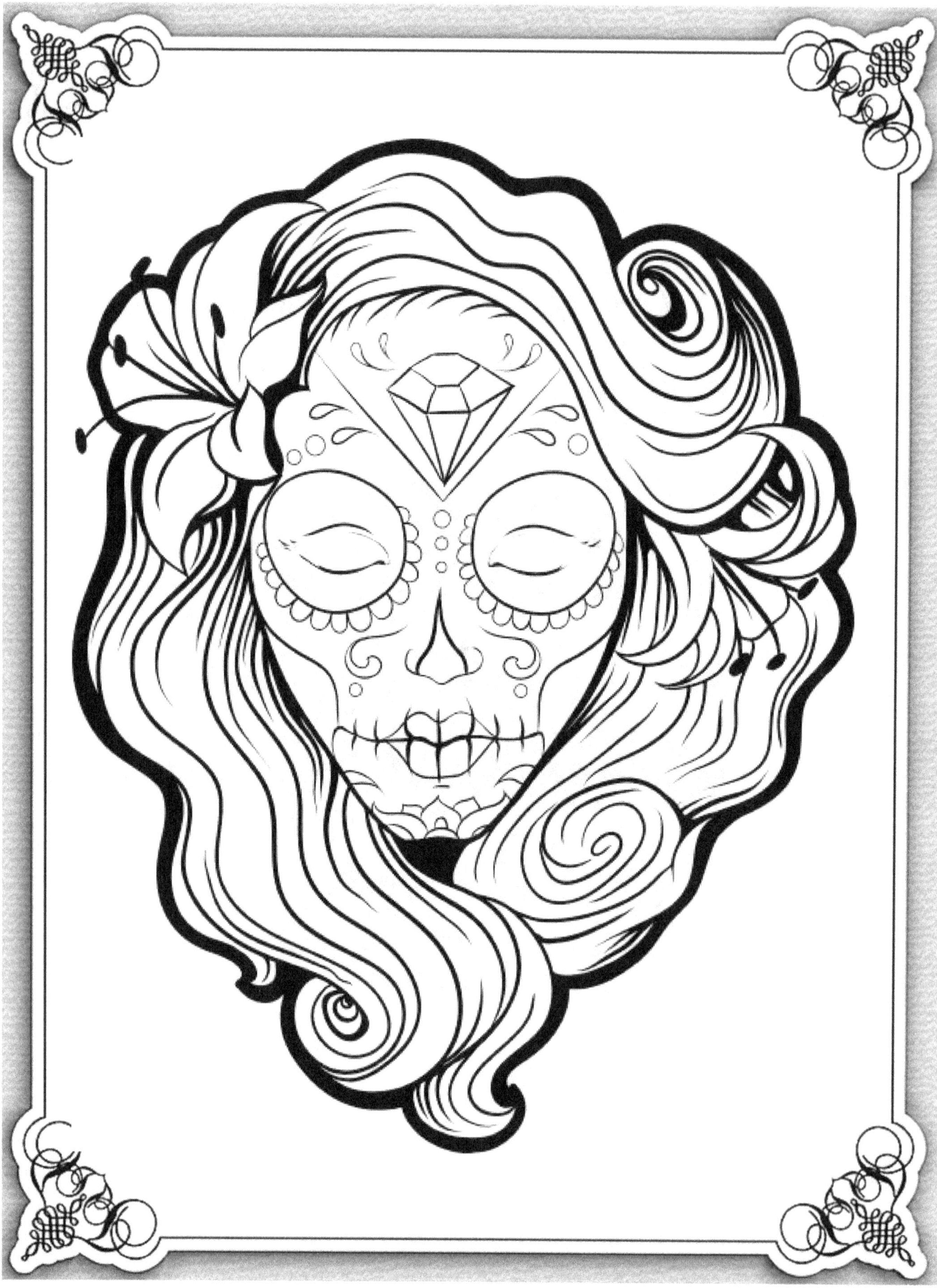

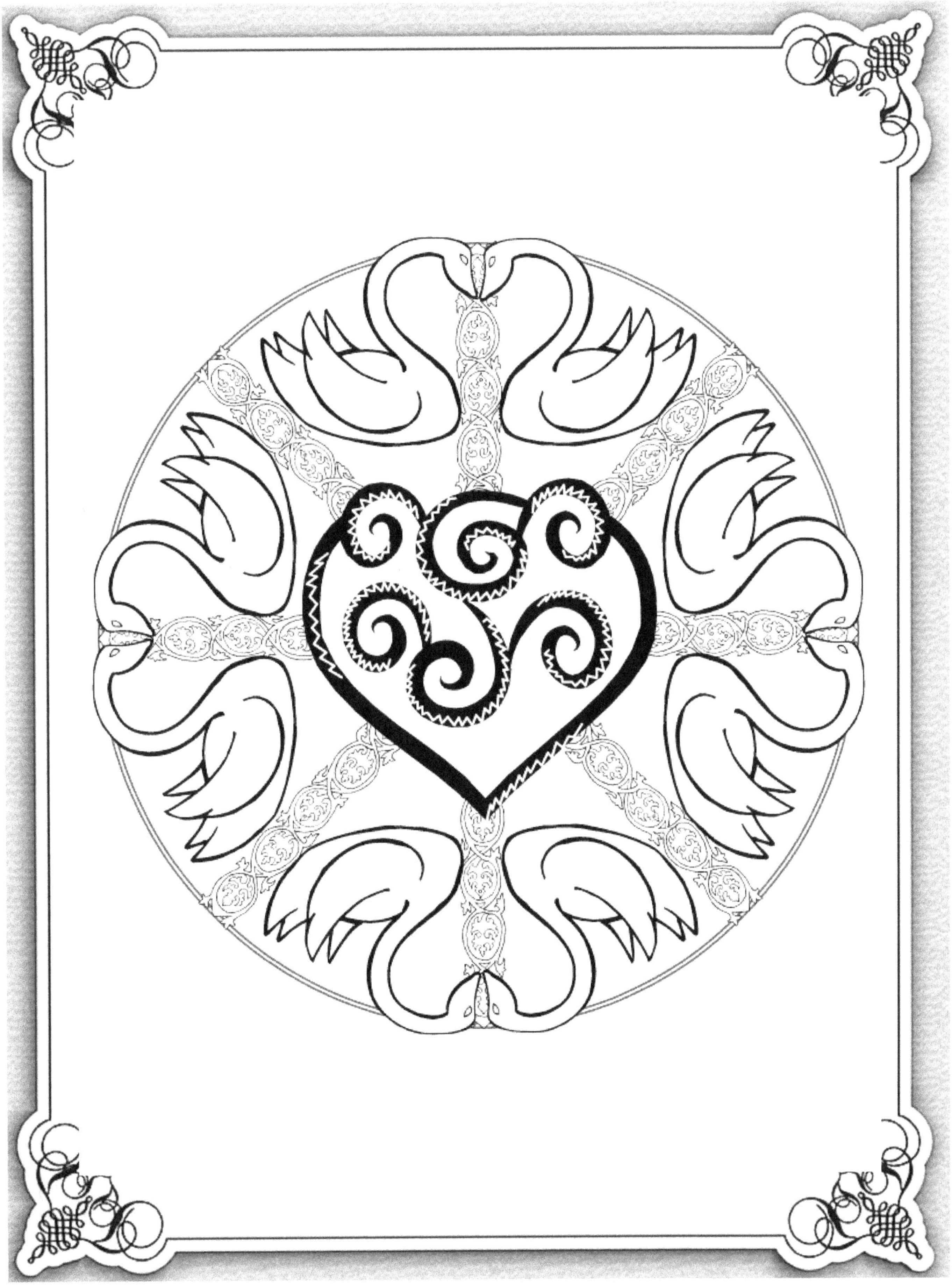

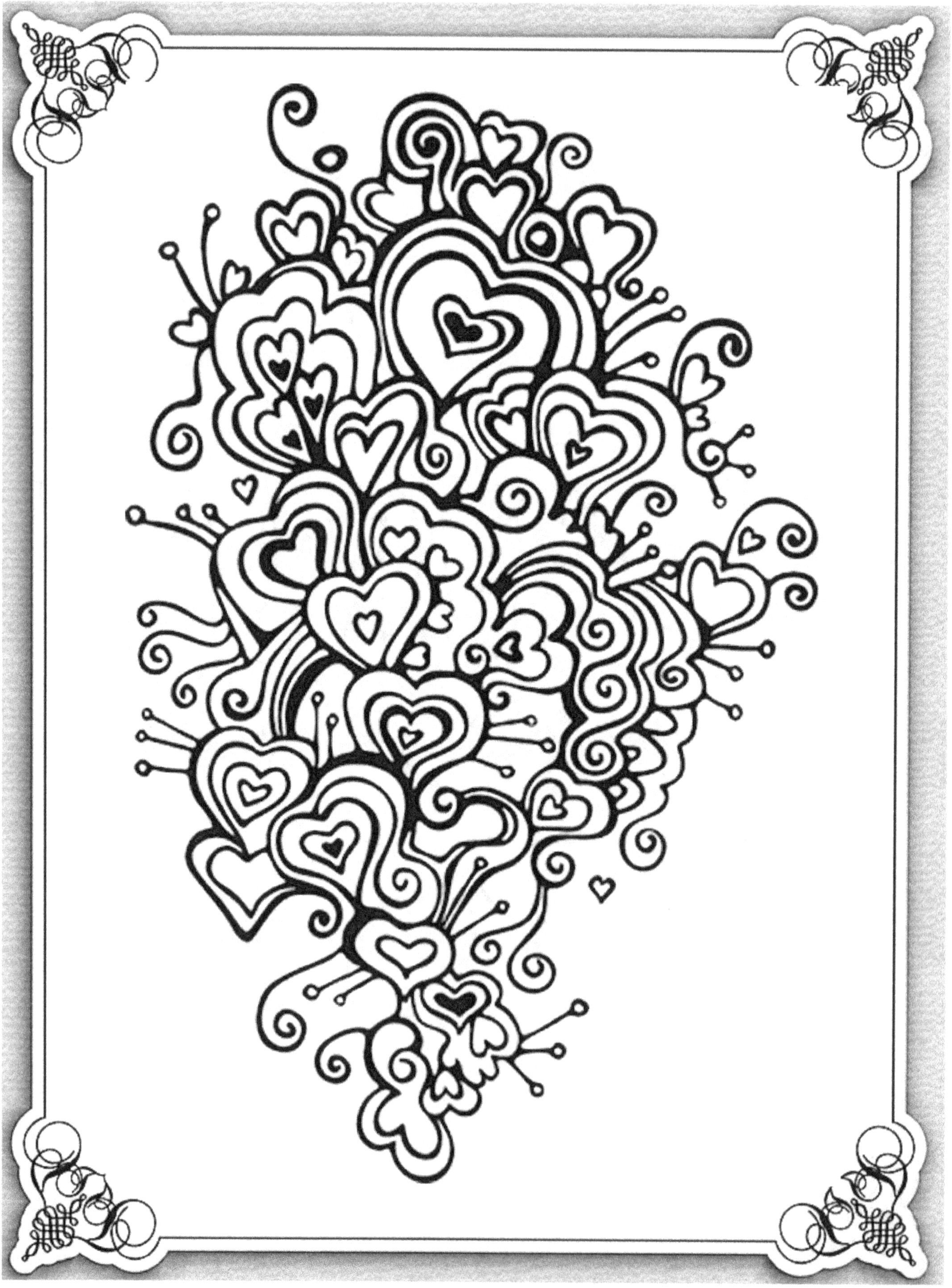

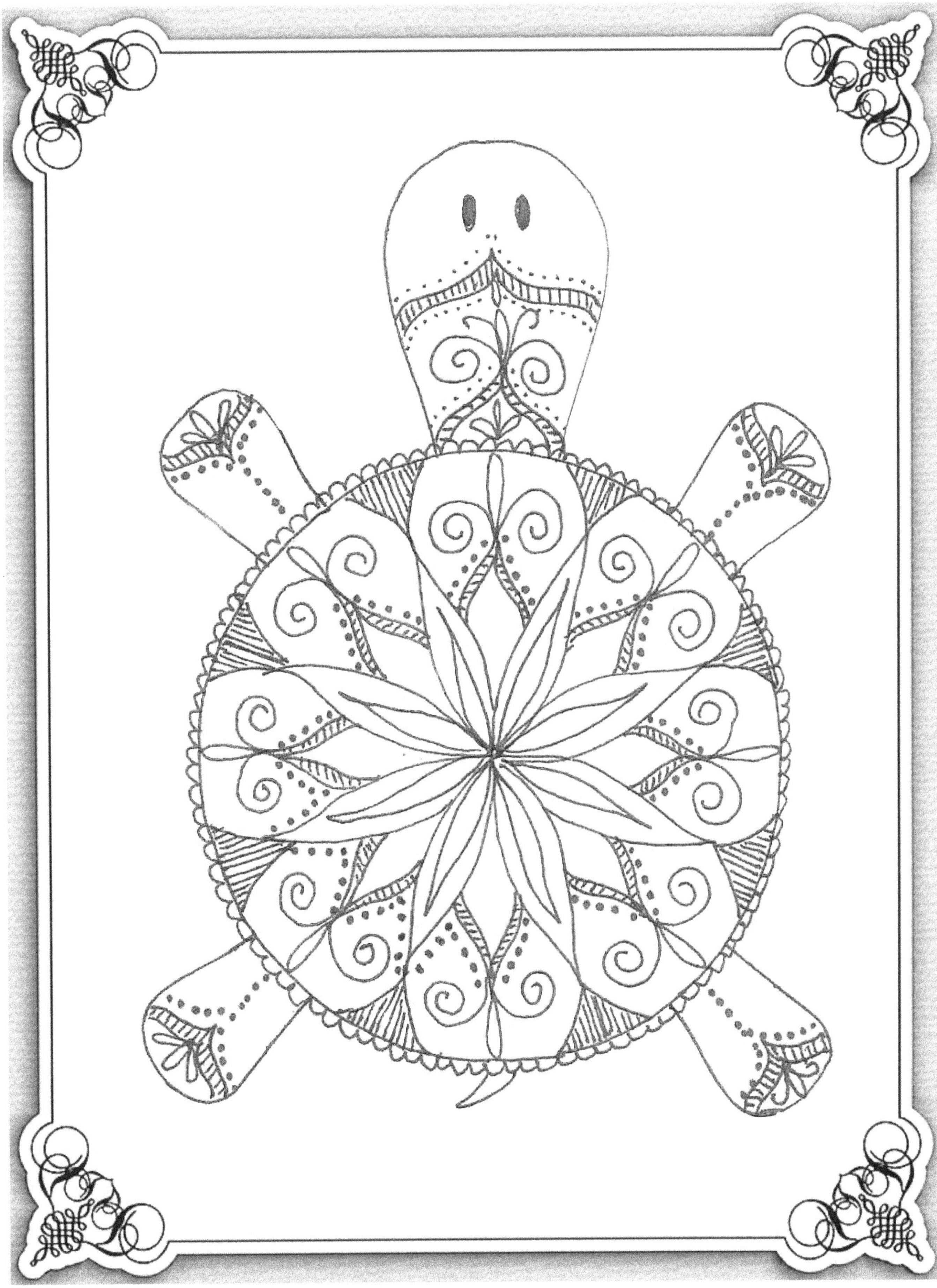

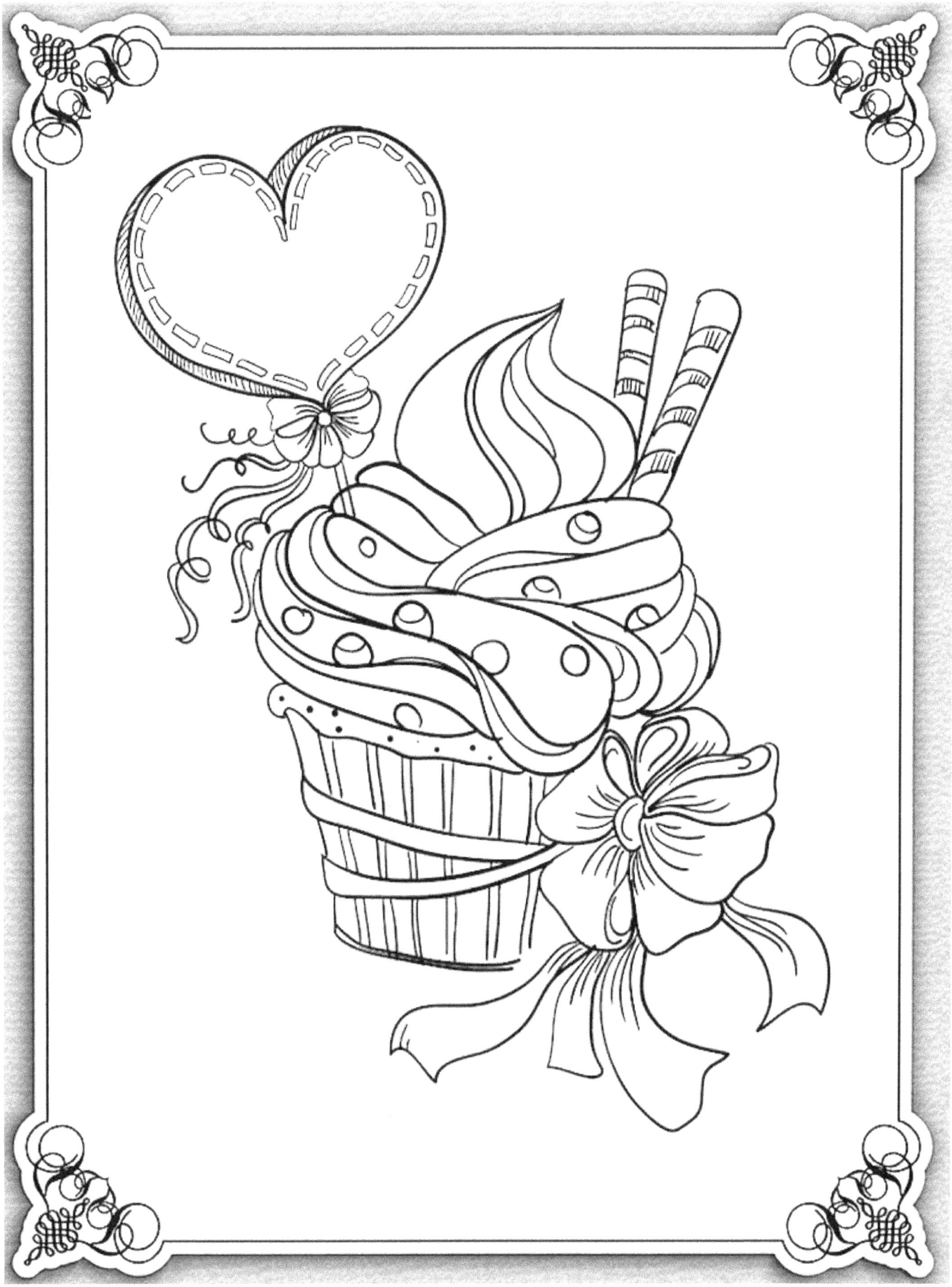

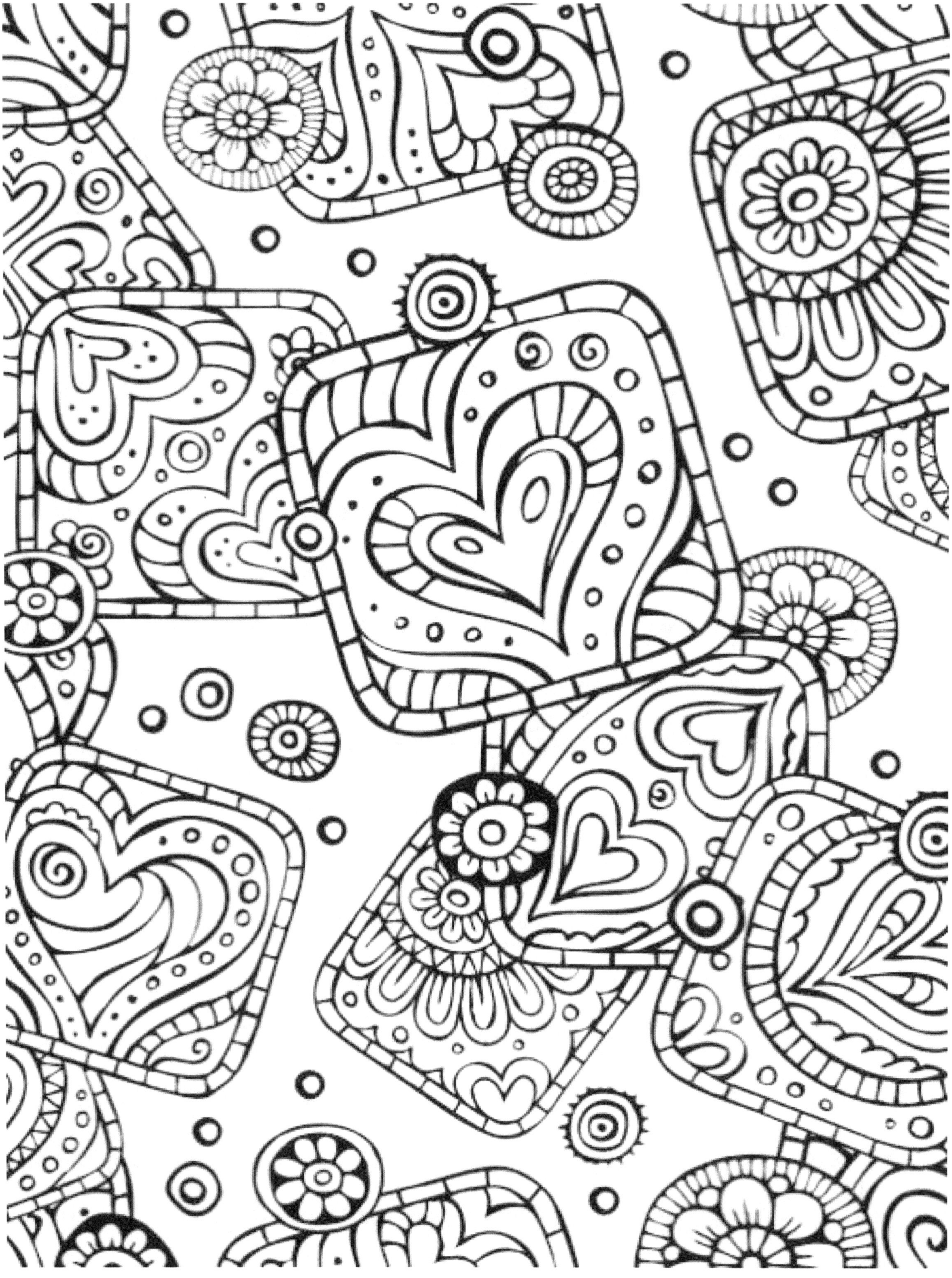

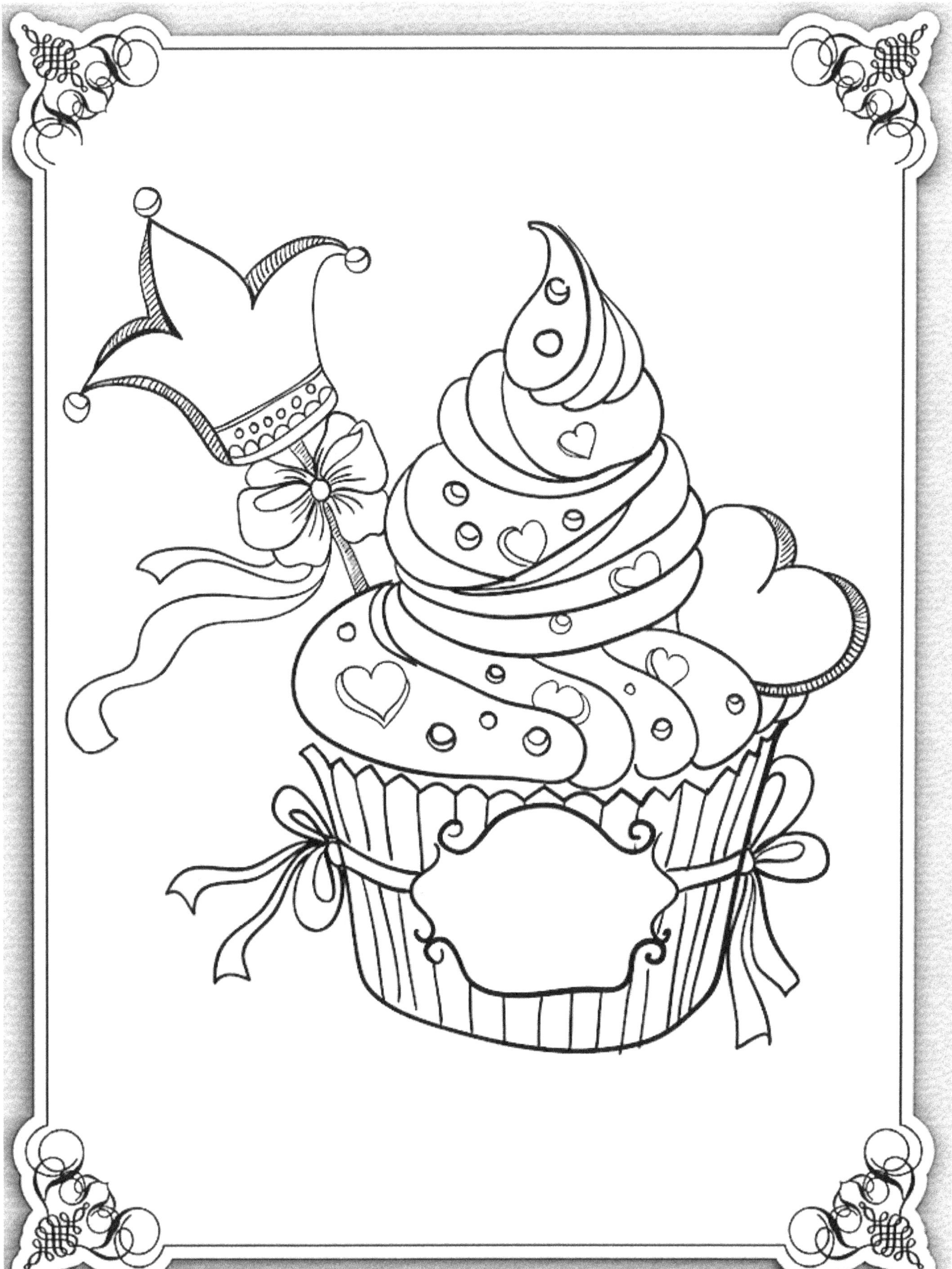

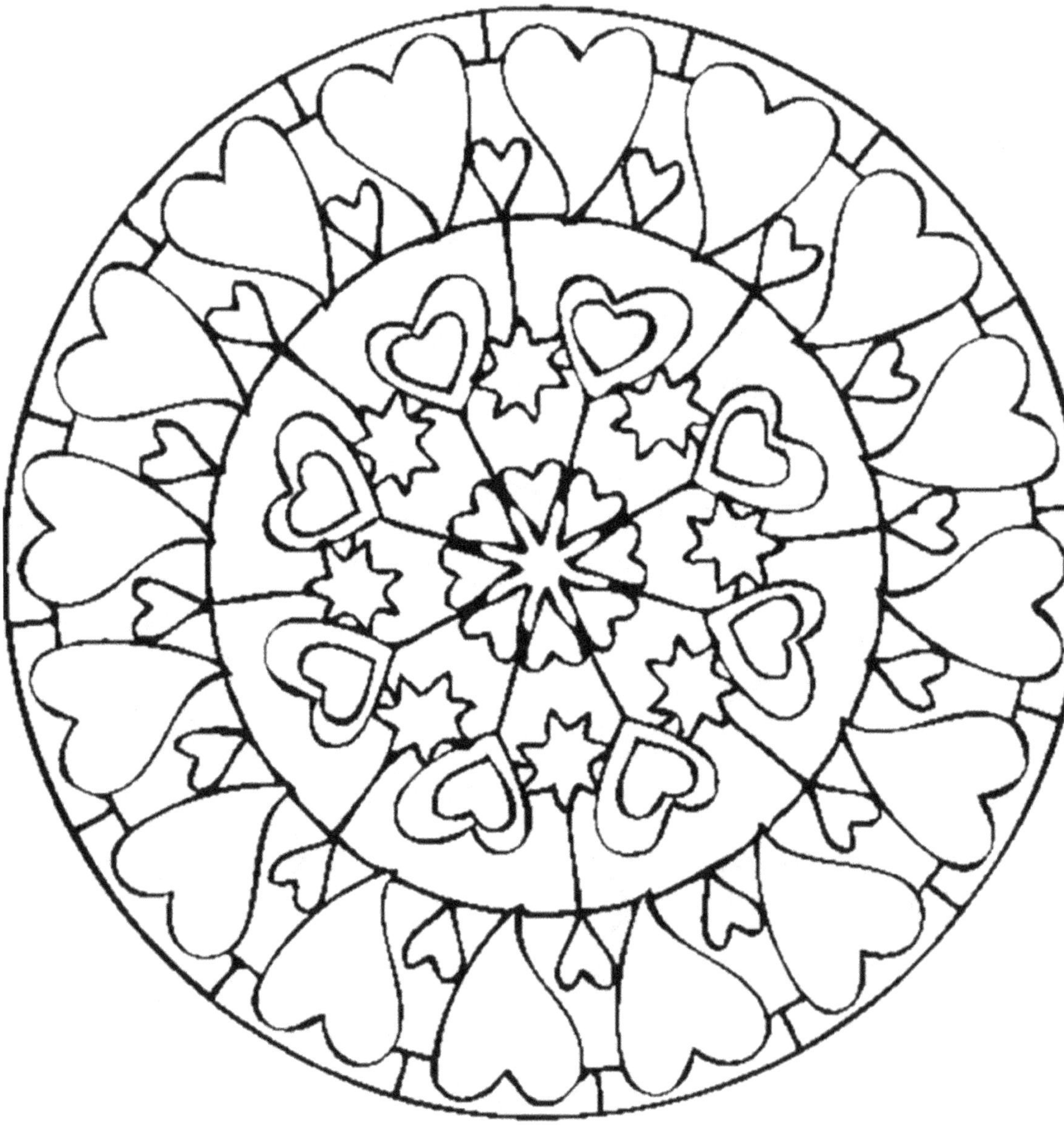

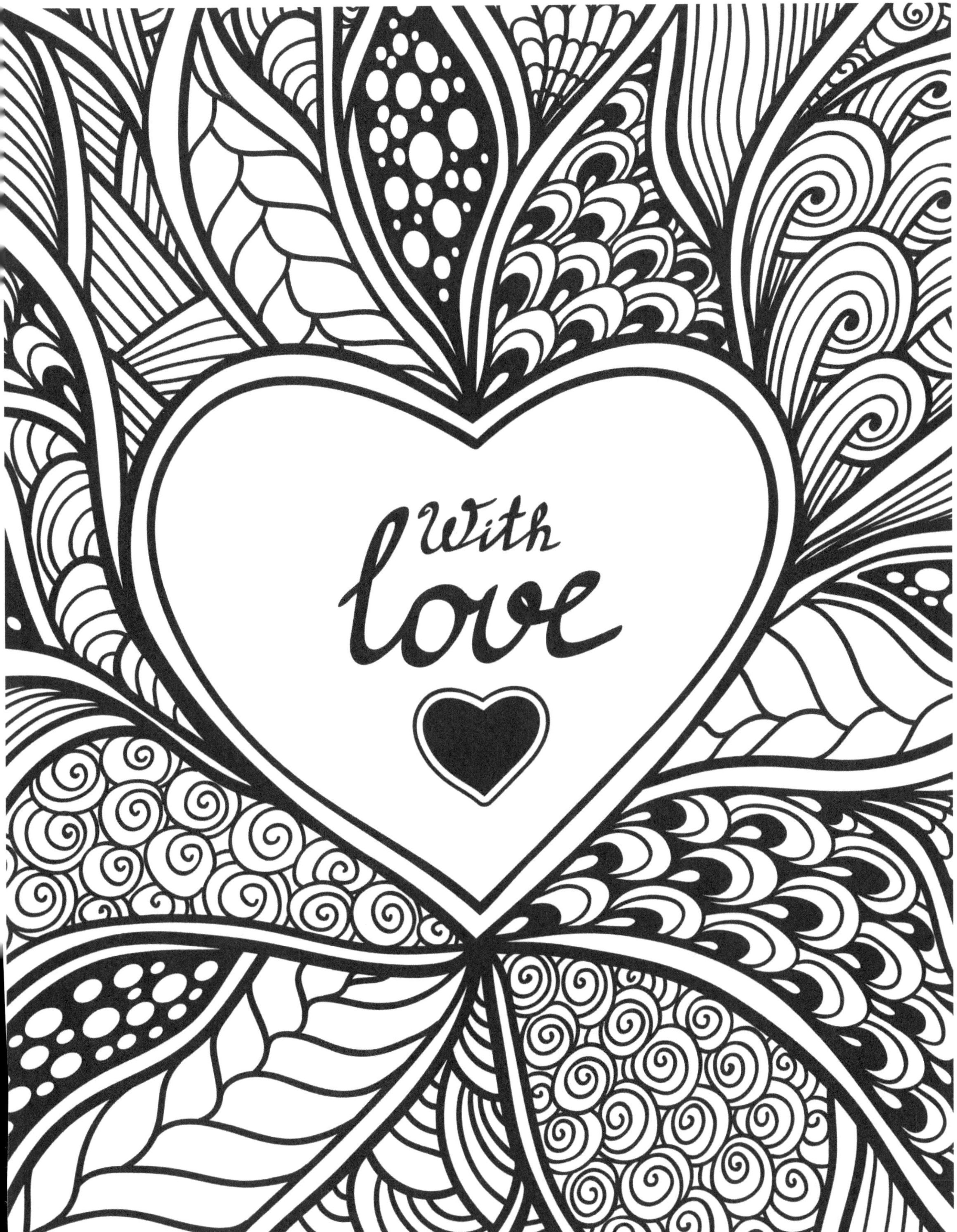
With
love

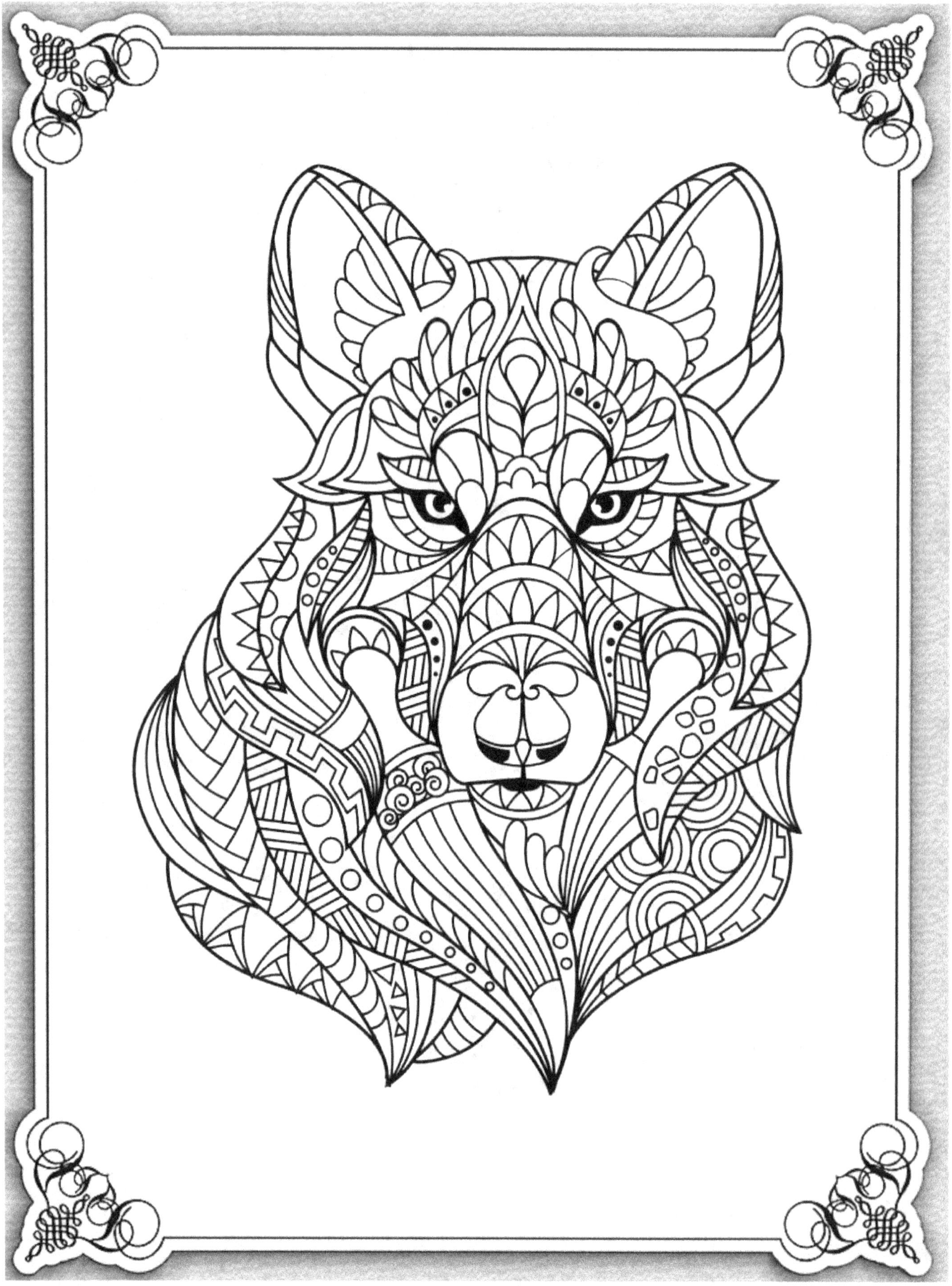

www.ingramcontent.com/pod-product-compliance
Lightning Source LLC
Chambersburg PA
CBHW080845220526
45467CB00008B/2399
9798683431457